Video Communication
Complete Self-Assessment Guide

The guidance in this Self-Assessment is based on Video Communication best practices and standards in business process architecture, design and quality management. The guidance is also based on the professional judgment of the individual collaborators listed in the Acknowledgments.

Notice of rights

Trademarks

Table of Contents

4

About The Art of Service

The Art of Service, Business Process Architects since 2000, is dedicated to helping stakeholders achieve excellence.

Defining, designing, creating, and implementing a process to solve a stakeholders challenge or meet an objective is the most valuable role... In EVERY group, company, organization and department.

Unless you're talking a one-time, single-use project, there should be a process. Whether that process is managed and implemented by humans, AI, or a combination of the two, it needs to be designed by someone with a complex enough perspective to ask the right questions.

Someone capable of asking the right questions and step back and say, 'What are we really trying to accomplish here? And is there a different way to look at it?'

With The Art of Service's Standard Requirements Self-Assessments, we empower people who can do just that — whether their title is marketer, entrepreneur, manager, salesperson, consultant, Business Process Manager, executive assistant, IT Manager, CIO etc... —they are the people who rule the future. They are people who watch the process as it happens, and ask the right questions to make the process work better.

Contact us when you need any support with this Self-Assessment and any help with templates, blue-prints and examples of standard documents you might need:

http://theartofservice.com
service@theartofservice.com

Included Resources - how to access

Included with your purchase of the book is the Video

Communication Self-Assessment Spreadsheet Dashboard which contains all questions and Self-Assessment areas and auto-generates insights, graphs, and project RACI planning - all with examples to get you started right away.

How? Simply send an email to
access@theartofservice.com
with this books' title in the subject to get the Video Communication Self Assessment Tool right away.

You will receive the following contents with New and Updated specific criteria:

- The latest quick edition of the book in PDF

- The latest complete edition of the book in PDF, which criteria correspond to the criteria in...

- The Self-Assessment Excel Dashboard, and...

- Example pre-filled Self-Assessment Excel Dashboard to get familiar with results generation

- In-depth specific Checklists covering the topic

- Project management checklists and templates to assist with implementation

INCLUDES LIFETIME SELF ASSESSMENT UPDATES

Every self assessment comes with Lifetime Updates and Lifetime Free Updated Books. Lifetime Updates is an industry-first feature which allows you to receive verified self assessment updates, ensuring you always have the most accurate information at your fingertips.

Get it now- you will be glad you did - do it now, before you forget.

Send an email to **access@theartofservice.com** with this books' title in the subject to get the Video Communication Self Assessment Tool right away.

Purpose of this Self-Assessment

This Self-Assessment has been developed to improve understanding of the requirements and elements of Video Communication, based on best practices and standards in business process architecture, design and quality management.

It is designed to allow for a rapid Self-Assessment to determine how closely existing management practices and procedures correspond to the elements of the Self-Assessment.

The criteria of requirements and elements of Video Communication have been rephrased in the format of a Self-Assessment questionnaire, with a seven-criterion scoring system, as explained in this document.

In this format, even with limited background knowledge of Video Communication, a manager can quickly review existing operations to determine how they measure up to the standards. This in turn can serve as the starting point of a 'gap analysis' to identify management tools or system elements that might usefully be implemented in the organization to help improve overall performance.

How to use the Self-Assessment

On the following pages are a series of questions to identify to what extent your Video Communication initiative is complete in comparison to the requirements set in standards.

To facilitate answering the questions, there is a space in front of each question to enter a score on a scale of '1' to '5'.

1 Strongly Disagree

2 Disagree

3 Neutral

4 Agree

5 Strongly Agree

Read the question and rate it with the following in front of mind:

'In my belief,
the answer to this question is clearly defined'.

There are two ways in which you can choose to interpret this statement;
1. how aware are you that the answer to the question is clearly defined
2. for more in-depth analysis you can choose to gather evidence and confirm the answer to the question. This obviously will take more time, most Self-Assessment users opt for the first way to interpret the question and dig deeper later on based on the outcome of the overall Self-Assessment.

A score of '1' would mean that the answer is not clear at all, where a '5' would mean the answer is crystal clear and defined. Leave emtpy when the question is not applicable or you don't want to answer it, you can skip it without affecting your score. Write your score in the space provided.

After you have responded to all the appropriate statements in each section, compute your average score for that section, using the formula provided, and round to the nearest tenth. Then transfer to the corresponding spoke in the Video Communication Scorecard on the second next page of the Self-Assessment.

Your completed Video Communication Scorecard will give you a clear presentation of which Video Communication areas need attention.

Video Communication
Scorecard Example

Example of how the finalized Scorecard can look like:

Video Communication Scorecard

Your Scores:

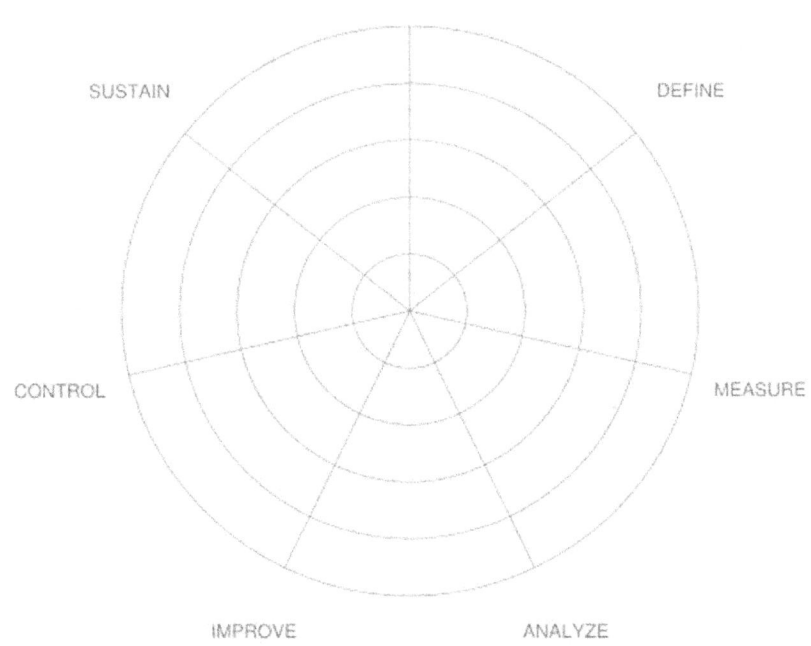

BEGINNING OF THE SELF-ASSESSMENT:

CRITERION #1: RECOGNIZE

INTENT: Be aware of the need for change. Recognize that there is an unfavorable variation, problem or symptom.

In my belief, the answer to this question is clearly defined:

5 Strongly Agree

4 Agree

3 Neutral

2 Disagree

1 Strongly Disagree

1. Which issues are too important to ignore?
<--- Score

2. Does your organization need more video communication education?
<--- Score

3. What information do users need?
<--- Score

4. Are losses recognized in a timely manner?
<--- Score

5. Is it clear when you think of the day ahead of you what activities and tasks you need to complete?
<--- Score

6. Is the need for organizational change recognized?
<--- Score

7. What are the timeframes required to resolve each of the issues/problems?
<--- Score

8. What video communication events should you attend?
<--- Score

9. Are there any specific expectations or concerns about the video communication team, video communication itself?
<--- Score

10. Will a response program recognize when a crisis occurs and provide some level of response?
<--- Score

11. How do you recognize an objection?
<--- Score

12. Did you miss any major video communication issues?
<--- Score

13. Do you have/need 24-hour access to key personnel?
<--- Score

14. Will it solve real problems?
<--- Score

15. Do you need different information or graphics?
<--- Score

16. To what extent does each concerned units management team recognize video communication as an effective investment?
<--- Score

17. Are there any revenue recognition issues?
<--- Score

18. How are training requirements identified?
<--- Score

19. Are you dealing with any of the same issues today as yesterday? What can you do about this?
<--- Score

20. Are employees recognized or rewarded for performance that demonstrates the highest levels of integrity?
<--- Score

21. How does it fit into your organizational needs and tasks?
<--- Score

22. Why is this needed?

<--- Score

23. What is the extent or complexity of the video communication problem?
<--- Score

24. What problems are you facing and how do you consider video communication will circumvent those obstacles?
<--- Score

25. Does video communication create potential expectations in other areas that need to be recognized and considered?
<--- Score

26. What extra resources will you need?
<--- Score

27. Are there video communication problems defined?
<--- Score

28. Who needs budgets?
<--- Score

29. Are there regulatory / compliance issues?
<--- Score

30. Is it needed?
<--- Score

31. For your video communication project, identify and describe the business environment, is there more than one layer to the business environment?
<--- Score

32. What does video communication success mean to the stakeholders?
<--- Score

33. What video communication capabilities do you need?
<--- Score

34. How do you take a forward-looking perspective in identifying video communication research related to market response and models?
<--- Score

35. Which needs are not included or involved?
<--- Score

36. To what extent would your organization benefit from being recognized as a award recipient?
<--- Score

37. Consider your own video communication project, what types of organizational problems do you think might be causing or affecting your problem, based on the work done so far?
<--- Score

38. What are the clients issues and concerns?
<--- Score

39. What is the problem and/or vulnerability?
<--- Score

40. What would happen if video communication weren't done?
<--- Score

41. What is the video communication problem definition? What do you need to resolve?
<--- Score

42. Have you identified your video communication key performance indicators?
<--- Score

43. What are the expected benefits of video communication to the stakeholder?
<--- Score

44. Whom do you really need or want to serve?
<--- Score

45. Who needs to know about video communication?
<--- Score

46. Do you need to avoid or amend any video communication activities?
<--- Score

47. What else needs to be measured?
<--- Score

48. How many trainings, in total, are needed?
<--- Score

49. How can auditing be a preventative security measure?
<--- Score

50. What are the stakeholder objectives to be achieved with video communication?

<--- Score

51. What resources or support might you need?
<--- Score

52. Who needs what information?
<--- Score

53. What training and capacity building actions are needed to implement proposed reforms?
<--- Score

54. Are controls defined to recognize and contain problems?
<--- Score

55. How much are sponsors, customers, partners, stakeholders involved in video communication? In other words, what are the risks, if video communication does not deliver successfully?
<--- Score

56. How do you recognize an video communication objection?
<--- Score

57. Are employees recognized for desired behaviors?
<--- Score

58. What creative shifts do you need to take?
<--- Score

59. What do employees need in the short term?
<--- Score

60. What is the problem or issue?

<--- Score

61. Who else hopes to benefit from it?
<--- Score

62. Think about the people you identified for your video communication project and the project responsibilities you would assign to them, what kind of training do you think they would need to perform these responsibilities effectively?
<--- Score

63. What vendors make products that address the video communication needs?
<--- Score

64. Why the need?
<--- Score

65. Can management personnel recognize the monetary benefit of video communication?
<--- Score

66. What is the recognized need?
<--- Score

67. What do you need to start doing?
<--- Score

68. Where is training needed?
<--- Score

69. Will video communication deliverables need to be tested and, if so, by whom?
<--- Score

70. What are the video communication resources needed?

<--- Score

71. What activities does the governance board need to consider?

<--- Score

72. What are your needs in relation to video communication skills, labor, equipment, and markets?

<--- Score

73. Looking at each person individually – does every one have the qualities which are needed to work in this group?

<--- Score

74. Do you recognize video communication achievements?

<--- Score

75. What video communication coordination do you need?

<--- Score

76. How do you assess your video communication workforce capability and capacity needs, including skills, competencies, and staffing levels?

<--- Score

77. How are you going to measure success?

<--- Score

78. Who are your key stakeholders who need to sign off?

<--- Score

79. When a video communication manager recognizes a problem, what options are available?
<--- Score

80. Which information does the video communication business case need to include?
<--- Score

81. Who needs to know?
<--- Score

82. What prevents you from making the changes you know will make you a more effective video communication leader?
<--- Score

83. What situation(s) led to this video communication Self Assessment?
<--- Score

84. How do you identify the kinds of information that you will need?
<--- Score

85. Does the problem have ethical dimensions?
<--- Score

86. What are the minority interests and what amount of minority interests can be recognized?
<--- Score

87. What is the smallest subset of the problem you can usefully solve?
<--- Score

88. What needs to be done?
<--- Score

89. How are the video communication's objectives aligned to the group's overall stakeholder strategy?
<--- Score

90. What tools and technologies are needed for a custom video communication project?
<--- Score

91. Do you know what you need to know about video communication?
<--- Score

92. What should be considered when identifying available resources, constraints, and deadlines?
<--- Score

93. What video communication problem should be solved?
<--- Score

94. As a sponsor, customer or management, how important is it to meet goals, objectives?
<--- Score

95. Is the quality assurance team identified?
<--- Score

96. Are problem definition and motivation clearly presented?
<--- Score

97. Will new equipment/products be required to facilitate video communication delivery, for

example is new software needed?
<--- Score

98. Who should resolve the video communication issues?
<--- Score

Add up total points for this section:
_ _ _ _ _ = Total points for this section

Divided by: _ _ _ _ _ _ (number of
statements answered) = _ _ _ _ _ _
Average score for this section

Transfer your score to the video
communication Index at the beginning
of the Self-Assessment.

CRITERION #2: DEFINE:

INTENT: Formulate the stakeholder problem. Define the problem, needs and objectives.

In my belief, the answer to this question is clearly defined:

5 Strongly Agree

4 Agree

3 Neutral

2 Disagree

1 Strongly Disagree

1. Is video communication linked to key stakeholder goals and objectives?
<--- Score

2. Does the team have regular meetings?
<--- Score

3. Who is gathering video communication information?

<--- Score

4. What key stakeholder process output measure(s) does video communication leverage and how?
<--- Score

5. What are the tasks and definitions?
<--- Score

6. What is in scope?
<--- Score

7. Is data collected and displayed to better understand customer(s) critical needs and requirements.
<--- Score

8. Are there different segments of customers?
<--- Score

9. Has/have the customer(s) been identified?
<--- Score

10. Has the improvement team collected the 'voice of the customer' (obtained feedback – qualitative and quantitative)?
<--- Score

11. Has anyone else (internal or external to the group) attempted to solve this problem or a similar one before? If so, what knowledge can be leveraged from these previous efforts?
<--- Score

12. How is the team tracking and documenting its work?
<--- Score

13. What are (control) requirements for video communication Information?
<--- Score

14. When is the estimated completion date?
<--- Score

15. What constraints exist that might impact the team?
<--- Score

16. What are the Roles and Responsibilities for each team member and its leadership? Where is this documented?
<--- Score

17. Has everyone on the team, including the team leaders, been properly trained?
<--- Score

18. What specifically is the problem? Where does it occur? When does it occur? What is its extent?
<--- Score

19. Are accountability and ownership for video communication clearly defined?
<--- Score

20. Are roles and responsibilities formally defined?
<--- Score

21. How does the video communication manager ensure against scope creep?
<--- Score

22. Do the problem and goal statements meet the SMART criteria (specific, measurable, attainable, relevant, and time-bound)?
<--- Score

23. Is full participation by members in regularly held team meetings guaranteed?
<--- Score

24. Why are you doing video communication and what is the scope?
<--- Score

25. Has the video communication work been fairly and/or equitably divided and delegated among team members who are qualified and capable to perform the work? Has everyone contributed?
<--- Score

26. How was the 'as is' process map developed, reviewed, verified and validated?
<--- Score

27. What is out-of-scope initially?
<--- Score

28. Is video communication required?
<--- Score

29. What would be the goal or target for a video communication's improvement team?
<--- Score

30. What are the core elements of the video communication business case?
<--- Score

31. How do you gather requirements?
<--- Score

32. What are the compelling stakeholder reasons for embarking on video communication?
<--- Score

33. In what way can you redefine the criteria of choice clients have in your category in your favor?
<--- Score

34. Is the scope of video communication defined?
<--- Score

35. Is there a video communication management charter, including stakeholder case, problem and goal statements, scope, milestones, roles and responsibilities, communication plan?
<--- Score

36. What information do you gather?
<--- Score

37. Has a team charter been developed and communicated?
<--- Score

38. What is out of scope?
<--- Score

39. What is the context?
<--- Score

40. What are the boundaries of the scope? What is in bounds and what is not? What is the start point? What

is the stop point?
<--- Score

41. Do you have organizational privacy requirements?
<--- Score

42. Is video communication currently on schedule according to the plan?
<--- Score

43. Is there a clear video communication case definition?
<--- Score

44. Is it clearly defined in and to your organization what you do?
<--- Score

45. What are the rough order estimates on cost savings/opportunities that video communication brings?
<--- Score

46. Are approval levels defined for contracts and supplements to contracts?
<--- Score

47. Will team members regularly document their video communication work?
<--- Score

48. Is the improvement team aware of the different versions of a process: what they think it is vs. what it actually is vs. what it should be vs. what it could be?
<--- Score

49. How would you define the culture at your organization, how susceptible is it to video communication changes?
<--- Score

50. Who defines (or who defined) the rules and roles?
<--- Score

51. When are meeting minutes sent out? Who is on the distribution list?
<--- Score

52. What defines best in class?
<--- Score

53. Is the work to date meeting requirements?
<--- Score

54. When is/was the video communication start date?
<--- Score

55. What customer feedback methods were used to solicit their input?
<--- Score

56. What baselines are required to be defined and managed?
<--- Score

57. Is the team adequately staffed with the desired cross-functionality? If not, what additional resources are available to the team?
<--- Score

58. The political context: who holds power?

<--- Score

59. What happens if video communication's scope changes?
<--- Score

60. What is the worst case scenario?
<--- Score

61. What are the video communication use cases?
<--- Score

62. What sources do you use to gather information for a video communication study?
<--- Score

63. Have specific policy objectives been defined?
<--- Score

64. How will the video communication team and the group measure complete success of video communication?
<--- Score

65. Are customer(s) identified and segmented according to their different needs and requirements?
<--- Score

66. Will team members perform video communication work when assigned and in a timely fashion?
<--- Score

67. Is there any additional video communication definition of success?
<--- Score

68. What is a worst-case scenario for losses?
<--- Score

69. What intelligence can you gather?
<--- Score

70. Is the team equipped with available and reliable resources?
<--- Score

71. How are consistent video communication definitions important?
<--- Score

72. How and when will the baselines be defined?
<--- Score

73. What is the definition of success?
<--- Score

74. How do you keep key subject matter experts in the loop?
<--- Score

75. Are the video communication requirements testable?
<--- Score

76. What scope to assess?
<--- Score

77. Where can you gather more information?
<--- Score

78. Is there a completed, verified, and validated high-level 'as is' (not 'should be' or 'could be') stakeholder

process map?

<--- Score

79. What are the dynamics of the communication plan?

<--- Score

80. Is special video communication user knowledge required?

<--- Score

81. How do you gather the stories?

<--- Score

82. Does the scope remain the same?

<--- Score

83. Are improvement team members fully trained on video communication?

<--- Score

84. Are all requirements met?

<--- Score

85. What are the record-keeping requirements of video communication activities?

<--- Score

86. Has your scope been defined?

<--- Score

87. What are the video communication tasks and definitions?

<--- Score

88. Will a video communication production

readiness review be required?
<--- Score

89. Has a high-level 'as is' process map been completed, verified and validated?
<--- Score

90. What video communication services do you require?
<--- Score

91. What is the definition of video communication excellence?
<--- Score

92. How often are the team meetings?
<--- Score

93. Do you have a video communication success story or case study ready to tell and share?
<--- Score

94. Scope of sensitive information?
<--- Score

95. Are task requirements clearly defined?
<--- Score

96. How do you build the right business case?
<--- Score

97. Has a project plan, Gantt chart, or similar been developed/completed?
<--- Score

98. Are there any constraints known that bear on the

ability to perform video communication work? How is the team addressing them?
<--- Score

99. What was the context?
<--- Score

100. Is the current 'as is' process being followed? If not, what are the discrepancies?
<--- Score

101. Is there a completed SIPOC representation, describing the Suppliers, Inputs, Process, Outputs, and Customers?
<--- Score

102. Are required metrics defined, what are they?
<--- Score

103. What video communication requirements should be gathered?
<--- Score

104. How do you hand over video communication context?
<--- Score

105. How do you think the partners involved in video communication would have defined success?
<--- Score

106. Is the video communication scope complete and appropriately sized?
<--- Score

107. Has a video communication requirement not

been met?
<--- Score

108. Have all basic functions of video communication been defined?
<--- Score

109. Have the customer needs been translated into specific, measurable requirements? How?
<--- Score

110. Is there regularly 100% attendance at the team meetings? If not, have appointed substitutes attended to preserve cross-functionality and full representation?
<--- Score

111. What is the scope of the video communication work?
<--- Score

112. Is the team formed and are team leaders (Coaches and Management Leads) assigned?
<--- Score

113. Is there a critical path to deliver video communication results?
<--- Score

114. Do you all define video communication in the same way?
<--- Score

115. How do you gather video communication requirements?
<--- Score

116. How do you catch video communication definition inconsistencies?
<--- Score

117. Have all of the relationships been defined properly?
<--- Score

118. What knowledge or experience is required?
<--- Score

119. How will variation in the actual durations of each activity be dealt with to ensure that the expected video communication results are met?
<--- Score

120. What is in the scope and what is not in scope?
<--- Score

121. Who are the video communication improvement team members, including Management Leads and Coaches?
<--- Score

122. If substitutes have been appointed, have they been briefed on the video communication goals and received regular communications as to the progress to date?
<--- Score

123. Is the video communication scope manageable?
<--- Score

124. Are audit criteria, scope, frequency and methods defined?

<--- Score

125. Are different versions of process maps needed to account for the different types of inputs?
<--- Score

126. How did the video communication manager receive input to the development of a video communication improvement plan and the estimated completion dates/times of each activity?
<--- Score

127. Who is gathering information?
<--- Score

128. What critical content must be communicated – who, what, when, where, and how?
<--- Score

129. How do you manage changes in video communication requirements?
<--- Score

130. What gets examined?
<--- Score

131. What system do you use for gathering video communication information?
<--- Score

132. How can the value of video communication be defined?
<--- Score

133. What are the requirements for audit information?
<--- Score

134. Are the video communication requirements complete?
<--- Score

135. Are resources adequate for the scope?
<--- Score

136. What is the scope of the video communication effort?
<--- Score

137. Has the direction changed at all during the course of video communication? If so, when did it change and why?
<--- Score

138. How do you manage unclear video communication requirements?
<--- Score

139. How do you manage scope?
<--- Score

140. How would you define video communication leadership?
<--- Score

141. What information should you gather?
<--- Score

Add up total points for this section:
_ _ _ _ _ = Total points for this section

Divided by: _ _ _ _ _ _ (number of statements answered) = _ _ _ _ _ _

Average score for this section

Transfer your score to the video
communication Index at the beginning
of the Self-Assessment.

CRITERION #3: MEASURE:

INTENT: Gather the correct data.
Measure the current performance and
evolution of the situation.

In my belief, the answer to this
question is clearly defined:

5 Strongly Agree

4 Agree

3 Neutral

2 Disagree

1 Strongly Disagree

1. Are actual costs in line with budgeted costs?
<--- Score

2. What are predictive video communication
analytics?
<--- Score

3. What measurements are possible, practicable and
meaningful?

<--- Score

4. Why do the measurements/indicators matter?
<--- Score

5. What is your decision requirements diagram?
<--- Score

6. What are your key video communication organizational performance measures, including key short and longer-term financial measures?
<--- Score

7. Do you effectively measure and reward individual and team performance?
<--- Score

8. Are the units of measure consistent?
<--- Score

9. Do the benefits outweigh the costs?
<--- Score

10. Is the solution cost-effective?
<--- Score

11. Which video communication impacts are significant?
<--- Score

12. How do you verify video communication completeness and accuracy?
<--- Score

13. Among the video communication product and service cost to be estimated, which is considered

hardest to estimate?
<--- Score

14. How do you stay flexible and focused to recognize larger video communication results?
<--- Score

15. Are video communication vulnerabilities categorized and prioritized?
<--- Score

16. Does management have the right priorities among projects?
<--- Score

17. Was a business case (cost/benefit) developed?
<--- Score

18. What could cause delays in the schedule?
<--- Score

19. What is the cost of rework?
<--- Score

20. Are there any easy-to-implement alternatives to video communication? Sometimes other solutions are available that do not require the cost implications of a full-blown project?
<--- Score

21. What causes mismanagement?
<--- Score

22. How frequently do you track video communication measures?
<--- Score

23. How do you verify the video communication requirements quality?

<--- Score

24. What are the costs and benefits?

<--- Score

25. What are the operational costs after video communication deployment?

<--- Score

26. How do you quantify and qualify impacts?

<--- Score

27. What are the estimated costs of proposed changes?

<--- Score

28. Are missed video communication opportunities costing your organization money?

<--- Score

29. What causes extra work or rework?

<--- Score

30. How do you verify performance?

<--- Score

31. Are indirect costs charged to the video communication program?

<--- Score

32. Do you have an issue in getting priority?

<--- Score

33. Did you tackle the cause or the symptom?
<--- Score

34. Where can you go to verify the info?
<--- Score

35. Does the video communication task fit the client's priorities?
<--- Score

36. What causes investor action?
<--- Score

37. How are measurements made?
<--- Score

38. How do you aggregate measures across priorities?
<--- Score

39. What are the video communication investment costs?
<--- Score

40. What are allowable costs?
<--- Score

41. What are the costs?
<--- Score

42. Which measures and indicators matter?
<--- Score

43. What methods are feasible and acceptable to estimate the impact of reforms?
<--- Score

44. Will video communication have an impact on current business continuity, disaster recovery processes and/or infrastructure?
<--- Score

45. What is your video communication quality cost segregation study?
<--- Score

46. How can you reduce the costs of obtaining inputs?
<--- Score

47. Where is the cost?
<--- Score

48. Is the cost worth the video communication effort ?
<--- Score

49. How is the value delivered by video communication being measured?
<--- Score

50. How can you manage cost down?
<--- Score

51. How will measures be used to manage and adapt?
<--- Score

52. How is performance measured?
<--- Score

53. What harm might be caused?
<--- Score

54. Who pays the cost?
<--- Score

55. What happens if cost savings do not materialize?
<--- Score

56. What details are required of the video communication cost structure?
<--- Score

57. Who should receive measurement reports?
<--- Score

58. How do you prevent mis-estimating cost?
<--- Score

59. What is the total cost related to deploying video communication, including any consulting or professional services?
<--- Score

60. What does losing customers cost your organization?
<--- Score

61. How will you measure success?
<--- Score

62. What drives O&M cost?
<--- Score

63. What relevant entities could be measured?
<--- Score

64. What are your customers expectations and

measures?
<--- Score

65. Are the video communication benefits worth its costs?
<--- Score

66. How do you focus on what is right -not who is right?
<--- Score

67. What is the root cause(s) of the problem?
<--- Score

68. How sensitive must the video communication strategy be to cost?
<--- Score

69. What would it cost to replace your technology?
<--- Score

70. How can you measure the performance?
<--- Score

71. How do you verify if video communication is built right?
<--- Score

72. What does your operating model cost?
<--- Score

73. Does a video communication quantification method exist?
<--- Score

74. How do you measure variability?

<--- Score

75. What is an unallowable cost?
<--- Score

76. What is your cost benefit analysis?
<--- Score

77. What evidence is there and what is measured?
<--- Score

78. Are you aware of what could cause a problem?
<--- Score

79. Is there an opportunity to verify requirements?
<--- Score

80. What users will be impacted?
<--- Score

81. What does verifying compliance entail?
<--- Score

82. What do you measure and why?
<--- Score

83. How can you measure video communication in a systematic way?
<--- Score

84. When a disaster occurs, who gets priority?
<--- Score

85. How to cause the change?
<--- Score

86. What could cause you to change course?
<--- Score

87. How much does it cost?
<--- Score

88. How frequently do you verify your video communication strategy?
<--- Score

89. How are you verifying it?
<--- Score

90. What are the video communication key cost drivers?
<--- Score

91. What are the costs of delaying video communication action?
<--- Score

92. How are costs allocated?
<--- Score

93. Are you taking your company in the direction of better and revenue or cheaper and cost?
<--- Score

94. What are you verifying?
<--- Score

95. Are the measurements objective?
<--- Score

96. What are your operating costs?
<--- Score

97. Do you have any cost video communication limitation requirements?
<--- Score

98. How do you control the overall costs of your work processes?
<--- Score

99. Are there measurements based on task performance?
<--- Score

100. How will the video communication data be analyzed?
<--- Score

101. The approach of traditional video communication works for detail complexity but is focused on a systematic approach rather than an understanding of the nature of systems themselves, what approach will permit your organization to deal with the kind of unpredictable emergent behaviors that dynamic complexity can introduce?
<--- Score

102. Do you verify that corrective actions were taken?
<--- Score

103. What are the uncertainties surrounding estimates of impact?
<--- Score

104. Which costs should be taken into account?
<--- Score

105. Have design-to-cost goals been established?
<--- Score

106. What is the video communication business impact?
<--- Score

107. How do you verify the authenticity of the data and information used?
<--- Score

108. Where is it measured?
<--- Score

109. How can a video communication test verify your ideas or assumptions?
<--- Score

110. What are hidden video communication quality costs?
<--- Score

111. How can you reduce costs?
<--- Score

112. When should you bother with diagrams?
<--- Score

113. How will your organization measure success?
<--- Score

114. What is the total fixed cost?
<--- Score

115. Is a follow-up focused external video communication review required?

<--- Score

116. What is measured? Why?
<--- Score

117. How is progress measured?
<--- Score

118. How do you measure lifecycle phases?
<--- Score

119. How do you verify and validate the video communication data?
<--- Score

120. What does a Test Case verify?
<--- Score

121. What are the costs of reform?
<--- Score

122. Are supply costs steady or fluctuating?
<--- Score

123. How long to keep data and how to manage retention costs?
<--- Score

124. Do you have a flow diagram of what happens?
<--- Score

125. Have you included everything in your video communication cost models?
<--- Score

126. Is it possible to estimate the impact of

unanticipated complexity such as wrong or failed assumptions, feedback, etcetera on proposed reforms?

<--- Score

127. How do you measure efficient delivery of video communication services?

<--- Score

128. What are your primary costs, revenues, assets?

<--- Score

129. Who is involved in verifying compliance?

<--- Score

130. How will success or failure be measured?

<--- Score

131. How will costs be allocated?

<--- Score

132. What causes innovation to fail or succeed in your organization?

<--- Score

133. What potential environmental factors impact the video communication effort?

<--- Score

134. What do people want to verify?

<--- Score

135. At what cost?

<--- Score

136. How do your measurements capture actionable video communication information for use in exceeding your customers expectations and securing your customers engagement?
<--- Score

137. Do you aggressively reward and promote the people who have the biggest impact on creating excellent video communication services/products?
<--- Score

138. When are costs are incurred?
<--- Score

139. What tests verify requirements?
<--- Score

140. How do you verify your resources?
<--- Score

141. What is the cause of any video communication gaps?
<--- Score

Add up total points for this section:
_ _ _ _ _ = Total points for this section

Divided by: _ _ _ _ _ _ (number of statements answered) = _ _ _ _ _ _
Average score for this section

Transfer your score to the video communication Index at the beginning of the Self-Assessment.

CRITERION #4: ANALYZE:

INTENT: Analyze causes, assumptions and hypotheses.

In my belief, the answer to this question is clearly defined:

5 Strongly Agree

4 Agree

3 Neutral

2 Disagree

1 Strongly Disagree

1. What is the complexity of the output produced?
<--- Score

2. Should you invest in industry-recognized qualifications?
<--- Score

3. How is video communication data gathered?
<--- Score

4. What other organizational variables, such as reward systems or communication systems, affect the performance of this video communication process?

<--- Score

5. How much data can be collected in the given timeframe?

<--- Score

6. What video communication metrics are outputs of the process?

<--- Score

7. How is the data gathered?

<--- Score

8. What is the oversight process?

<--- Score

9. Are video communication changes recognized early enough to be approved through the regular process?

<--- Score

10. Is data and process analysis, root cause analysis and quantifying the gap/opportunity in place?

<--- Score

11. Is there any way to speed up the process?

<--- Score

12. What are your best practices for minimizing video communication project risk, while demonstrating incremental value and quick wins throughout the video communication project lifecycle?

<--- Score

13. What are the personnel training and qualifications required?
<--- Score

14. How will corresponding data be collected?
<--- Score

15. Do your leaders quickly bounce back from setbacks?
<--- Score

16. Who is involved in the management review process?
<--- Score

17. What are evaluation criteria for the output?
<--- Score

18. What kind of crime could a potential new hire have committed that would not only not disqualify him/her from being hired by your organization, but would actually indicate that he/she might be a particularly good fit?
<--- Score

19. What tools were used to narrow the list of possible causes?
<--- Score

20. Is the final output clearly identified?
<--- Score

21. Were Pareto charts (or similar) used to portray the 'heavy hitters' (or key sources of variation)?

<--- Score

22. What is your organizations process which leads to recognition of value generation?
<--- Score

23. How was the detailed process map generated, verified, and validated?
<--- Score

24. What data is gathered?
<--- Score

25. What internal processes need improvement?
<--- Score

26. Were any designed experiments used to generate additional insight into the data analysis?
<--- Score

27. How do you implement and manage your work processes to ensure that they meet design requirements?
<--- Score

28. What is the cost of poor quality as supported by the team's analysis?
<--- Score

29. What are your current levels and trends in key measures or indicators of video communication product and process performance that are important to and directly serve your customers? How do these results compare with the performance of your competitors and other organizations with similar offerings?

<--- Score

30. What are your key performance measures or indicators and in-process measures for the control and improvement of your video communication processes?
<--- Score

31. Have the problem and goal statements been updated to reflect the additional knowledge gained from the analyze phase?
<--- Score

32. Do your contracts/agreements contain data security obligations?
<--- Score

33. What are the disruptive video communication technologies that enable your organization to radically change your business processes?
<--- Score

34. Are your outputs consistent?
<--- Score

35. What are the video communication business drivers?
<--- Score

36. Where is video communication data gathered?
<--- Score

37. Who is involved with workflow mapping?
<--- Score

38. Was a cause-and-effect diagram used to explore

the different types of causes (or sources of variation)?
<--- Score

39. Do you, as a leader, bounce back quickly from setbacks?
<--- Score

40. What process improvements will be needed?
<--- Score

41. What methods do you use to gather video communication data?
<--- Score

42. What are the necessary qualifications?
<--- Score

43. What does the data say about the performance of the stakeholder process?
<--- Score

44. Did any value-added analysis or 'lean thinking' take place to identify some of the gaps shown on the 'as is' process map?
<--- Score

45. How do you ensure that the video communication opportunity is realistic?
<--- Score

46. What qualifications are needed?
<--- Score

47. Do quality systems drive continuous improvement?
<--- Score

48. What did the team gain from developing a sub-process map?
<--- Score

49. How is the way you as the leader think and process information affecting your organizational culture?
<--- Score

50. Record-keeping requirements flow from the records needed as inputs, outputs, controls and for transformation of a video communication process, are the records needed as inputs to the video communication process available?
<--- Score

51. An organizationally feasible system request is one that considers the mission, goals and objectives of the organization, key questions are: is the video communication solution request practical and will it solve a problem or take advantage of an opportunity to achieve company goals?
<--- Score

52. What is your organizations system for selecting qualified vendors?
<--- Score

53. Is the video communication process severely broken such that a re-design is necessary?
<--- Score

54. What data do you need to collect?
<--- Score

55. How often will data be collected for measures?

<--- Score

56. Which video communication data should be retained?
<--- Score

57. What is the output?
<--- Score

58. What video communication data will be collected?
<--- Score

59. How has the video communication data been gathered?
<--- Score

60. What are your outputs?
<--- Score

61. How do you define collaboration and team output?
<--- Score

62. How will the change process be managed?
<--- Score

63. What process should you select for improvement?
<--- Score

64. What qualifications do video communication leaders need?
<--- Score

65. Who will facilitate the team and process?
<--- Score

66. What controls do you have in place to protect data?
<--- Score

67. How do your work systems and key work processes relate to and capitalize on your core competencies?
<--- Score

68. What resources go in to get the desired output?
<--- Score

69. Did any additional data need to be collected?
<--- Score

70. Is the performance gap determined?
<--- Score

71. What are your video communication processes?
<--- Score

72. What, related to, video communication processes does your organization outsource?
<--- Score

73. When should a process be art not science?
<--- Score

74. Is the gap/opportunity displayed and communicated in financial terms?
<--- Score

75. What video communication data should be managed?

<--- Score

76. How do you use video communication data and information to support organizational decision making and innovation?
<--- Score

77. Have any additional benefits been identified that will result from closing all or most of the gaps?
<--- Score

78. Is there a strict change management process?
<--- Score

79. Where is the data coming from to measure compliance?
<--- Score

80. Are all staff in core video communication subjects Highly Qualified?
<--- Score

81. Do your employees have the opportunity to do what they do best everyday?
<--- Score

82. What systems/processes must you excel at?
<--- Score

83. Can you add value to the current video communication decision-making process (largely qualitative) by incorporating uncertainty modeling (more quantitative)?
<--- Score

84. What are the processes for audit reporting and

management?
<--- Score

85. Are gaps between current performance and the goal performance identified?
<--- Score

86. What training and qualifications will you need?
<--- Score

87. Are all team members qualified for all tasks?
<--- Score

88. What video communication data do you gather or use now?
<--- Score

89. What conclusions were drawn from the team's data collection and analysis? How did the team reach these conclusions?
<--- Score

90. What information qualified as important?
<--- Score

91. Is the suppliers process defined and controlled?
<--- Score

92. What qualifications and skills do you need?
<--- Score

93. How are outputs preserved and protected?
<--- Score

94. What is the Value Stream Mapping?

<--- Score

95. Do staff qualifications match your project?
<--- Score

96. Is the required video communication data gathered?
<--- Score

97. Is pre-qualification of suppliers carried out?
<--- Score

98. What tools were used to generate the list of possible causes?
<--- Score

99. Were there any improvement opportunities identified from the process analysis?
<--- Score

100. What other jobs or tasks affect the performance of the steps in the video communication process?
<--- Score

101. What output to create?
<--- Score

102. How many input/output points does it require?
<--- Score

103. How do mission and objectives affect the video communication processes of your organization?
<--- Score

104. How does the organization define, manage, and improve its video communication processes?
<--- Score

105. What qualifications are necessary?
<--- Score

106. Has an output goal been set?
<--- Score

107. Who will gather what data?
<--- Score

108. What are your current levels and trends in key video communication measures or indicators of product and process performance that are important to and directly serve your customers?
<--- Score

109. Who owns what data?
<--- Score

110. Was a detailed process map created to amplify critical steps of the 'as is' stakeholder process?
<--- Score

111. Do you understand your management processes today?
<--- Score

112. Where can you get qualified talent today?
<--- Score

113. What are the revised rough estimates of the financial savings/opportunity for video

communication improvements?
<--- Score

114. What were the financial benefits resulting from any 'ground fruit or low-hanging fruit' (quick fixes)?
<--- Score

115. What types of data do your video communication indicators require?
<--- Score

116. Has data output been validated?
<--- Score

117. What qualifies as competition?
<--- Score

118. What were the crucial 'moments of truth' on the process map?
<--- Score

119. What is the video communication Driver?
<--- Score

120. What successful thing are you doing today that may be blinding you to new growth opportunities?
<--- Score

121. Think about some of the processes you undertake within your organization, which do you own?
<--- Score

122. What do you need to qualify?
<--- Score

123. How do you identify specific video communication investment opportunities and emerging trends?

<--- Score

124. What quality tools were used to get through the analyze phase?

<--- Score

125. What video communication data should be collected?

<--- Score

126. What will drive video communication change?

<--- Score

127. Who gets your output?

<--- Score

128. Are you missing video communication opportunities?

<--- Score

129. Identify an operational issue in your organization, for example, could a particular task be done more quickly or more efficiently by video communication?

<--- Score

130. How do you measure the operational performance of your key work systems and processes, including productivity, cycle time, and other appropriate measures of process effectiveness, efficiency, and innovation?

<--- Score

131. Is there an established change management process?
<--- Score

Add up total points for this section:
_____ = Total points for this section

Divided by: _____ (number of statements answered) = _____
Average score for this section

Transfer your score to the video communication Index at the beginning of the Self-Assessment.

CRITERION #5: IMPROVE:

INTENT: Develop a practical solution. Innovate, establish and test the solution and to measure the results.

In my belief, the answer to this question is clearly defined:

5 Strongly Agree

4 Agree

3 Neutral

2 Disagree

1 Strongly Disagree

1. Who controls the risk?
<--- Score

2. How does the team improve its work?
<--- Score

3. Have you achieved video communication improvements?
<--- Score

4. What assumptions are made about the solution and approach?
<--- Score

5. Are risk triggers captured?
<--- Score

6. Is a solution implementation plan established, including schedule/work breakdown structure, resources, risk management plan, cost/budget, and control plan?
<--- Score

7. Is the scope clearly documented?
<--- Score

8. Will the controls trigger any other risks?
<--- Score

9. How do you measure risk?
<--- Score

10. Are decisions made in a timely manner?
<--- Score

11. To what extent does management recognize video communication as a tool to increase the results?
<--- Score

12. What alternative responses are available to manage risk?
<--- Score

13. Why improve in the first place?
<--- Score

14. How do you define the solutions' scope?
<--- Score

15. Where do you need video communication improvement?
<--- Score

16. Are the most efficient solutions problem-specific?
<--- Score

17. How will you recognize and celebrate results?
<--- Score

18. What risks do you need to manage?
<--- Score

19. What improvements have been achieved?
<--- Score

20. Is video communication documentation maintained?
<--- Score

21. Is a contingency plan established?
<--- Score

22. Risk Identification: What are the possible risk events your organization faces in relation to video communication?
<--- Score

23. What do you want to improve?
<--- Score

24. Risk events: what are the things that could go

wrong?
<--- Score

25. Have you identified breakpoints and/or risk tolerances that will trigger broad consideration of a potential need for intervention or modification of strategy?
<--- Score

26. Risk factors: what are the characteristics of video communication that make it risky?
<--- Score

27. Who are the video communication decision-makers?
<--- Score

28. How will you measure the results?
<--- Score

29. Do you combine technical expertise with business knowledge and video communication Key topics include lifecycles, development approaches, requirements and how to make a business case?
<--- Score

30. Is any video communication documentation required?
<--- Score

31. Who controls key decisions that will be made?
<--- Score

32. When you map the key players in your own work and the types/domains of relationships with them, which relationships do you find easy and which

challenging, and why?
<--- Score

33. What area needs the greatest improvement?
<--- Score

34. Is the video communication risk managed?
<--- Score

35. What is the implementation plan?
<--- Score

36. Who will be responsible for documenting the video communication requirements in detail?
<--- Score

37. Is the implementation plan designed?
<--- Score

38. Who are the video communication decision makers?
<--- Score

39. How do you improve video communication service perception, and satisfaction?
<--- Score

40. Who manages supplier risk management in your organization?
<--- Score

41. What current systems have to be understood and/ or changed?
<--- Score

42. How are video communication risks managed?

<--- Score

43. Was a video communication charter developed?
<--- Score

44. Who makes the video communication decisions in your organization?
<--- Score

45. For estimation problems, how do you develop an estimation statement?
<--- Score

46. Who are the key stakeholders for the video communication evaluation?
<--- Score

47. What actually has to improve and by how much?
<--- Score

48. What tools were used to tap into the creativity and encourage 'outside the box' thinking?
<--- Score

49. Do those selected for the video communication team have a good general understanding of what video communication is all about?
<--- Score

50. How can you improve video communication?
<--- Score

51. Are events managed to resolution?
<--- Score

52. Are the risks fully understood, reasonable and manageable?
<--- Score

53. How does your organization evaluate strategic video communication success?
<--- Score

54. Which of the recognised risks out of all risks can be most likely transferred?
<--- Score

55. What to do with the results or outcomes of measurements?
<--- Score

56. Is there any other video communication solution?
<--- Score

57. What criteria will you use to assess your video communication risks?
<--- Score

58. What were the underlying assumptions on the cost-benefit analysis?
<--- Score

59. How will you know when its improved?
<--- Score

60. Were any criteria developed to assist the team in testing and evaluating potential solutions?
<--- Score

61. How do you manage and improve your video communication work systems to deliver customer

value and achieve organizational success and
sustainability?
<--- Score

62. What is the video communication's sustainability
risk?
<--- Score

63. Is the measure of success for video communication
understandable to a variety of people?
<--- Score

64. How risky is your organization?
<--- Score

65. How do you improve productivity?
<--- Score

**66. What resources are required for the
improvement efforts?**
<--- Score

**67. Is there a high likelihood that any
recommendations will achieve their intended
results?**
<--- Score

68. Are the key business and technology risks being
managed?
<--- Score

**69. Would you develop a video communication
Communication Strategy?**
<--- Score

70. Is the optimal solution selected based on testing

and analysis?
<--- Score

71. Is the video communication solution sustainable?
<--- Score

**72. What are the implications of the one critical
video communication decision 10 minutes, 10
months, and 10 years from now?**
<--- Score

73. How are policy decisions made and where?
<--- Score

74. Is there a cost/benefit analysis of optimal
solution(s)?
<--- Score

75. What went well, what should change, what can
improve?
<--- Score

76. Is supporting video communication
documentation required?
<--- Score

77. Do you need to do a usability evaluation?
<--- Score

78. Is the solution technically practical?
<--- Score

79. How do you mitigate video communication risk?
<--- Score

80. Who do you report video communication results

to?

<--- Score

81. How do you manage video communication risk?

<--- Score

82. What lessons, if any, from a pilot were incorporated into the design of the full-scale solution?

<--- Score

83. What video communication improvements can be made?

<--- Score

84. What attendant changes will need to be made to ensure that the solution is successful?

<--- Score

85. What are the concrete video communication results?

<--- Score

86. What are the expected video communication results?

<--- Score

87. What is video communication risk?

<--- Score

88. How do you measure progress and evaluate training effectiveness?

<--- Score

89. What should a proof of concept or pilot accomplish?

<--- Score

90. Which video communication solution is appropriate?
<--- Score

91. What are the video communication security risks?
<--- Score

92. Are you assessing video communication and risk?
<--- Score

93. How scalable is your video communication solution?
<--- Score

94. In the past few months, what is the smallest change you have made that has had the biggest positive result? What was it about that small change that produced the large return?
<--- Score

95. Where do the video communication decisions reside?
<--- Score

96. video communication risk decisions: whose call Is It?
<--- Score

97. For decision problems, how do you develop a decision statement?
<--- Score

98. How do you keep improving video communication?

<--- Score

99. What are the affordable video communication risks?
<--- Score

100. What were the criteria for evaluating a video communication pilot?
<--- Score

101. How do you link measurement and risk?
<--- Score

102. How do you decide how much to remunerate an employee?
<--- Score

103. How will you know that a change is an improvement?
<--- Score

104. How do you deal with video communication risk?
<--- Score

105. What strategies for video communication improvement are successful?
<--- Score

106. What practices helps your organization to develop its capacity to recognize patterns?
<--- Score

107. If you could go back in time five years, what decision would you make differently? What is your best guess as to what decision you're making today

you might regret five years from now?
<--- Score

108. What can you do to improve?
<--- Score

109. Is the video communication documentation thorough?
<--- Score

110. What does the 'should be' process map/design look like?
<--- Score

111. Who should make the video communication decisions?
<--- Score

112. Explorations of the frontiers of video communication will help you build influence, improve video communication, optimize decision making, and sustain change, what is your approach?
<--- Score

113. Do vendor agreements bring new compliance risk ?
<--- Score

114. Who will be responsible for making the decisions to include or exclude requested changes once video communication is underway?
<--- Score

115. How can the phases of video communication development be identified?
<--- Score

116. Who will be using the results of the measurement activities?
<--- Score

117. What needs improvement? Why?
<--- Score

118. What is the team's contingency plan for potential problems occurring in implementation?
<--- Score

119. How do you improve your likelihood of success ?
<--- Score

120. Are procedures documented for managing video communication risks?
<--- Score

121. Is risk periodically assessed?
<--- Score

122. What tools were used to evaluate the potential solutions?
<--- Score

123. How do the video communication results compare with the performance of your competitors and other organizations with similar offerings?
<--- Score

124. What is the magnitude of the improvements?
<--- Score

125. What error proofing will be done to address some

of the discrepancies observed in the 'as is' process?
<--- Score

126. At what point will vulnerability assessments be performed once video communication is put into production (e.g., ongoing Risk Management after implementation)?
<--- Score

127. Does the goal represent a desired result that can be measured?
<--- Score

128. Can you identify any significant risks or exposures to video communication third- parties (vendors, service providers, alliance partners etc) that concern you?
<--- Score

129. Do you have the optimal project management team structure?
<--- Score

130. What is video communication's impact on utilizing the best solution(s)?
<--- Score

131. How do you measure improved video communication service perception, and satisfaction?
<--- Score

132. Was a pilot designed for the proposed solution(s)?
<--- Score

133. Who are the people involved in developing

and implementing video communication?
<--- Score

134. What communications are necessary to support the implementation of the solution?
<--- Score

135. What is the risk?
<--- Score

136. Do you cover the five essential competencies: Communication, Collaboration,Innovation, Adaptability, and Leadership that improve an organizations ability to leverage the new video communication in a volatile global economy?
<--- Score

137. Is pilot data collected and analyzed?
<--- Score

138. Is there a small-scale pilot for proposed improvement(s)? What conclusions were drawn from the outcomes of a pilot?
<--- Score

139. What tools do you use once you have decided on a video communication strategy and more importantly how do you choose?
<--- Score

140. Does a good decision guarantee a good outcome?
<--- Score

141. What tools were most useful during the improve phase?

<--- Score

Add up total points for this section:
_ _ _ _ _ = Total points for this section

Divided by: _ _ _ _ _ _ (number of
statements answered) = _ _ _ _ _ _
Average score for this section

Transfer your score to the video
communication Index at the beginning
of the Self-Assessment.

CRITERION #6: CONTROL:

INTENT: Implement the practical solution. Maintain the performance and correct possible complications.

In my belief, the answer to this question is clearly defined:

5 Strongly Agree

4 Agree

3 Neutral

2 Disagree

1 Strongly Disagree

1. Has the improved process and its steps been standardized?
<--- Score

2. Are new process steps, standards, and documentation ingrained into normal operations?
<--- Score

3. How will report readings be checked to effectively

monitor performance?
<--- Score

4. Who sets the video communication standards?
<--- Score

5. What are your results for key measures or indicators of the accomplishment of your video communication strategy and action plans, including building and strengthening core competencies?
<--- Score

6. What adjustments to the strategies are needed?
<--- Score

7. How do you plan on providing proper recognition and disclosure of supporting companies?
<--- Score

8. Where do ideas that reach policy makers and planners as proposals for video communication strengthening and reform actually originate?
<--- Score

9. Does a troubleshooting guide exist or is it needed?
<--- Score

10. Against what alternative is success being measured?
<--- Score

11. How likely is the current video communication plan to come in on schedule or on budget?
<--- Score

12. What are the known security controls?

<--- Score

13. What are you attempting to measure/monitor?
<--- Score

14. Does the video communication performance meet the customer's requirements?
<--- Score

15. What is the standard for acceptable video communication performance?
<--- Score

16. How will you measure your QA plan's effectiveness?
<--- Score

17. Is there a documented and implemented monitoring plan?
<--- Score

18. Who has control over resources?
<--- Score

19. In the case of a video communication project, the criteria for the audit derive from implementation objectives, an audit of a video communication project involves assessing whether the recommendations outlined for implementation have been met, can you track that any video communication project is implemented as planned, and is it working?
<--- Score

20. What are customers monitoring?
<--- Score

21. How can you best use all of your knowledge repositories to enhance learning and sharing?
<--- Score

22. Is knowledge gained on process shared and institutionalized?
<--- Score

23. What are the key elements of your video communication performance improvement system, including your evaluation, organizational learning, and innovation processes?
<--- Score

24. Are suggested corrective/restorative actions indicated on the response plan for known causes to problems that might surface?
<--- Score

25. What other areas of the group might benefit from the video communication team's improvements, knowledge, and learning?
<--- Score

26. What are the critical parameters to watch?
<--- Score

27. Does video communication appropriately measure and monitor risk?
<--- Score

28. What is the recommended frequency of auditing?
<--- Score

29. Are the video communication standards

challenging?
<--- Score

30. How might the group capture best practices and lessons learned so as to leverage improvements?
<--- Score

31. Is there a video communication Communication plan covering who needs to get what information when?
<--- Score

32. How do you spread information?
<--- Score

33. Are pertinent alerts monitored, analyzed and distributed to appropriate personnel?
<--- Score

34. Are controls in place and consistently applied?
<--- Score

35. What should you measure to verify efficiency gains?
<--- Score

36. How will the process owner and team be able to hold the gains?
<--- Score

37. What do you measure to verify effectiveness gains?
<--- Score

38. Who controls critical resources?
<--- Score

39. Is there an action plan in case of emergencies?
<--- Score

40. How do you monitor usage and cost?
<--- Score

41. How do you select, collect, align, and integrate video communication data and information for tracking daily operations and overall organizational performance, including progress relative to strategic objectives and action plans?
<--- Score

42. What do you stand for--and what are you against?
<--- Score

43. Do the viable solutions scale to future needs?
<--- Score

44. Does job training on the documented procedures need to be part of the process team's education and training?
<--- Score

45. Are the planned controls in place?
<--- Score

46. Do the video communication decisions you make today help people and the planet tomorrow?
<--- Score

47. What is the control/monitoring plan?
<--- Score

48. How is change control managed?

<--- Score

49. What other systems, operations, processes, and infrastructures (hiring practices, staffing, training, incentives/rewards, metrics/dashboards/scorecards, etc.) need updates, additions, changes, or deletions in order to facilitate knowledge transfer and improvements?
<--- Score

50. Is there a recommended audit plan for routine surveillance inspections of video communication's gains?
<--- Score

51. How do you encourage people to take control and responsibility?
<--- Score

52. What key inputs and outputs are being measured on an ongoing basis?
<--- Score

53. What are the performance and scale of the video communication tools?
<--- Score

54. How will video communication decisions be made and monitored?
<--- Score

55. What video communication standards are applicable?
<--- Score

56. What can you control?

<--- Score

57. You may have created your quality measures at a time when you lacked resources, technology wasn't up to the required standard, or low service levels were the industry norm. Have those circumstances changed?
<--- Score

58. Will existing staff require re-training, for example, to learn new business processes?
<--- Score

59. Is a response plan in place for when the input, process, or output measures indicate an 'out-of-control' condition?
<--- Score

60. Is there a transfer of ownership and knowledge to process owner and process team tasked with the responsibilities.
<--- Score

61. Who is the video communication process owner?
<--- Score

62. What is your plan to assess your security risks?
<--- Score

63. Can you adapt and adjust to changing video communication situations?
<--- Score

64. Is a response plan established and deployed?
<--- Score

65. Are there documented procedures?
<--- Score

66. What is the best design framework for video communication organization now that, in a post industrial-age if the top-down, command and control model is no longer relevant?
<--- Score

67. Have new or revised work instructions resulted?
<--- Score

68. How will new or emerging customer needs/ requirements be checked/communicated to orient the process toward meeting the new specifications and continually reducing variation?
<--- Score

69. What should the next improvement project be that is related to video communication?
<--- Score

70. Will any special training be provided for results interpretation?
<--- Score

71. Do you monitor the effectiveness of your video communication activities?
<--- Score

72. Does the response plan contain a definite closed loop continual improvement scheme (e.g., plan-do-check-act)?
<--- Score

73. Is new knowledge gained imbedded in the

response plan?
<--- Score

74. How will input, process, and output variables be checked to detect for sub-optimal conditions?
<--- Score

75. How widespread is its use?
<--- Score

76. How do senior leaders actions reflect a commitment to the organizations video communication values?
<--- Score

77. What do your reports reflect?
<--- Score

78. Will your goals reflect your program budget?
<--- Score

79. Who is going to spread your message?
<--- Score

80. What is your theory of human motivation, and how does your compensation plan fit with that view?
<--- Score

81. How will the day-to-day responsibilities for monitoring and continual improvement be transferred from the improvement team to the process owner?
<--- Score

82. Do you monitor the video communication decisions made and fine tune them as they evolve?

<--- Score

83. Will the team be available to assist members in planning investigations?
<--- Score

84. Has the video communication value of standards been quantified?
<--- Score

85. Are operating procedures consistent?
<--- Score

86. How will the process owner verify improvement in present and future sigma levels, process capabilities?
<--- Score

87. How do you plan for the cost of succession?
<--- Score

88. Can support from partners be adjusted?
<--- Score

89. Is the video communication test/monitoring cost justified?
<--- Score

90. What quality tools were useful in the control phase?
<--- Score

91. Implementation Planning: is a pilot needed to test the changes before a full roll out occurs?
<--- Score

92. How do your controls stack up?

<--- Score

93. Is there a standardized process?
<--- Score

94. Is there a control plan in place for sustaining improvements (short and long-term)?
<--- Score

95. Is reporting being used or needed?
<--- Score

96. Are documented procedures clear and easy to follow for the operators?
<--- Score

97. Is there documentation that will support the successful operation of the improvement?
<--- Score

Add up total points for this section:
_____ = Total points for this section

Divided by: _____ (number of statements answered) = _____
Average score for this section

Transfer your score to the video communication Index at the beginning of the Self-Assessment.

CRITERION #7: SUSTAIN:

INTENT: Retain the benefits.

In my belief, the answer to this question is clearly defined:

5 Strongly Agree

4 Agree

3 Neutral

2 Disagree

1 Strongly Disagree

1. What trouble can you get into?
<--- Score

2. How do senior leaders deploy your organizations vision and values through your leadership system, to the workforce, to key suppliers and partners, and to customers and other stakeholders, as appropriate?
<--- Score

3. What is the overall talent health of your organization as a whole at senior levels, and for each

organization reporting to a member of the Senior Leadership Team?

<--- Score

4. How do customers see your organization?

<--- Score

5. What video communication modifications can you make work for you?

<--- Score

6. What are the potential basics of video communication fraud?

<--- Score

7. Which individuals, teams or departments will be involved in video communication?

<--- Score

8. If you weren't already in this business, would you enter it today? And if not, what are you going to do about it?

<--- Score

9. What are your most important goals for the strategic video communication objectives?

<--- Score

10. Is there a work around that you can use?

<--- Score

11. How do you lead with video communication in mind?

<--- Score

12. What video communication skills are most

important?
<--- Score

13. Who are the key stakeholders?
<--- Score

14. What is your formula for success in video communication ?
<--- Score

15. What are the long-term video communication goals?
<--- Score

16. Why is it important to have senior management support for a video communication project?
<--- Score

17. What stupid rule would you most like to kill?
<--- Score

18. Why should people listen to you?
<--- Score

19. What would have to be true for the option on the table to be the best possible choice?
<--- Score

20. How do you make it meaningful in connecting video communication with what users do day-to-day?
<--- Score

21. Why should you adopt a video communication framework?

<--- Score

22. How do you manage video communication Knowledge Management (KM)?
<--- Score

23. What are the challenges?
<--- Score

24. How will you ensure you get what you expected?
<--- Score

25. What have you done to protect your business from competitive encroachment?
<--- Score

26. Who will determine interim and final deadlines?
<--- Score

27. What are the key enablers to make this video communication move?
<--- Score

28. What is it like to work for you?
<--- Score

29. How do you foster the skills, knowledge, talents, attributes, and characteristics you want to have?
<--- Score

30. What goals did you miss?
<--- Score

31. Are the criteria for selecting recommendations stated?

<--- Score

32. If your company went out of business tomorrow, would anyone who doesn't get a paycheck here care?
<--- Score

33. What are the gaps in your knowledge and experience?
<--- Score

34. How do you keep records, of what?
<--- Score

35. Are there any activities that you can take off your to do list?
<--- Score

36. What are you trying to prove to yourself, and how might it be hijacking your life and business success?
<--- Score

37. What business benefits will video communication goals deliver if achieved?
<--- Score

38. How will you motivate the stakeholders with the least vested interest?
<--- Score

39. Which video communication goals are the most important?
<--- Score

40. Are all key stakeholders present at all Structured Walkthroughs?

<--- Score

41. What unique value proposition (UVP) do you offer?
<--- Score

42. Is your strategy driving your strategy? Or is the way in which you allocate resources driving your strategy?
<--- Score

43. Are assumptions made in video communication stated explicitly?
<--- Score

44. Who have you, as a company, historically been when you've been at your best?
<--- Score

45. What counts that you are not counting?
<--- Score

46. How are you doing compared to your industry?
<--- Score

47. What is your competitive advantage?
<--- Score

48. How do you engage the workforce, in addition to satisfying them?
<--- Score

49. What is something you believe that nearly no one agrees with you on?
<--- Score

50. What would you recommend your friend do if he/

she were facing this dilemma?
<--- Score

51. How do you stay inspired?
<--- Score

52. Do you have past video communication successes?
<--- Score

53. How do you track customer value, profitability or financial return, organizational success, and sustainability?
<--- Score

54. How do you create buy-in?
<--- Score

55. If you were responsible for initiating and implementing major changes in your organization, what steps might you take to ensure acceptance of those changes?
<--- Score

56. What is your video communication strategy?
<--- Score

57. If there were zero limitations, what would you do differently?
<--- Score

58. When information truly is ubiquitous, when reach and connectivity are completely global, when computing resources are infinite, and when a whole new set of impossibilities are not only possible, but happening, what will that do to your business?

<--- Score

59. Is video communication realistic, or are you setting yourself up for failure?
<--- Score

60. What are the short and long-term video communication goals?
<--- Score

61. Why do and why don't your customers like your organization?
<--- Score

62. Who will provide the final approval of video communication deliverables?
<--- Score

63. What should you stop doing?
<--- Score

64. Who is responsible for video communication?
<--- Score

65. Is there any reason to believe the opposite of my current belief?
<--- Score

66. How do you foster innovation?
<--- Score

67. How likely is it that a customer would recommend your company to a friend or colleague?
<--- Score

68. Do you think video communication accomplishes

the goals you expect it to accomplish?
<--- Score

69. How will you insure seamless interoperability of video communication moving forward?
<--- Score

70. Can the schedule be done in the given time?
<--- Score

71. What are your personal philosophies regarding video communication and how do they influence your work?
<--- Score

72. What information is critical to your organization that your executives are ignoring?
<--- Score

73. What could happen if you do not do it?
<--- Score

74. What are current video communication paradigms?
<--- Score

75. How do you go about securing video communication?
<--- Score

76. What is the source of the strategies for video communication strengthening and reform?
<--- Score

77. Is video communication dependent on the successful delivery of a current project?

<--- Score

78. What is the range of capabilities?
<--- Score

79. How do you proactively clarify deliverables and video communication quality expectations?
<--- Score

80. What one word do you want to own in the minds of your customers, employees, and partners?
<--- Score

81. What is the kind of project structure that would be appropriate for your video communication project, should it be formal and complex, or can it be less formal and relatively simple?
<--- Score

82. Is a video communication breakthrough on the horizon?
<--- Score

83. What does your signature ensure?
<--- Score

84. What are strategies for increasing support and reducing opposition?
<--- Score

85. What potential megatrends could make your business model obsolete?
<--- Score

86. Do you think you know, or do you know you

know ?
<--- Score

87. What you are going to do to affect the numbers?
<--- Score

88. What is the funding source for this project?
<--- Score

89. What may be the consequences for the performance of an organization if all stakeholders are not consulted regarding video communication?
<--- Score

90. What are the top 3 things at the forefront of your video communication agendas for the next 3 years?
<--- Score

91. What is your question? Why?
<--- Score

92. To whom do you add value?
<--- Score

93. How can you incorporate support to ensure safe and effective use of video communication into the services that you provide?
<--- Score

94. How do you set video communication stretch targets and how do you get people to not only participate in setting these stretch targets but also that they strive to achieve these?
<--- Score

95. Who is on the team?

<--- Score

96. Think of your video communication project, what are the main functions?
<--- Score

97. Operational - will it work?
<--- Score

98. Why will customers want to buy your organizations products/services?
<--- Score

99. Are you making progress, and are you making progress as video communication leaders?
<--- Score

100. How do you deal with video communication changes?
<--- Score

101. Why is video communication important for you now?
<--- Score

102. Is it economical; do you have the time and money?
<--- Score

103. What have been your experiences in defining long range video communication goals?
<--- Score

104. How will you know that the video communication project has been successful?
<--- Score

105. What are the success criteria that will indicate that video communication objectives have been met and the benefits delivered?
<--- Score

106. What is your BATNA (best alternative to a negotiated agreement)?
<--- Score

107. What happens when a new employee joins the organization?
<--- Score

108. What is the recommended frequency of auditing?
<--- Score

109. Can you maintain your growth without detracting from the factors that have contributed to your success?
<--- Score

110. Are the assumptions believable and achievable?
<--- Score

111. What is effective video communication?
<--- Score

112. What will be the consequences to the stakeholder (financial, reputation etc) if video communication does not go ahead or fails to deliver the objectives?
<--- Score

113. How do you maintain video communication's

Integrity?
<--- Score

114. What projects are going on in the organization today, and what resources are those projects using from the resource pools?
<--- Score

115. Ask yourself: how would you do this work if you only had one staff member to do it?
<--- Score

116. Instead of going to current contacts for new ideas, what if you reconnected with dormant contacts--the people you used to know? If you were going reactivate a dormant tie, who would it be?
<--- Score

117. Are you maintaining a past–present–future perspective throughout the video communication discussion?
<--- Score

118. Who else should you help?
<--- Score

119. What is a feasible sequencing of reform initiatives over time?
<--- Score

120. Who is the main stakeholder, with ultimate responsibility for driving video communication forward?
<--- Score

121. What trophy do you want on your mantle?

<--- Score

122. What happens at your organization when people fail?
<--- Score

123. Is a video communication team work effort in place?
<--- Score

124. How much contingency will be available in the budget?
<--- Score

125. Which models, tools and techniques are necessary?
<--- Score

126. Who uses your product in ways you never expected?
<--- Score

127. What is the overall business strategy?
<--- Score

128. Whose voice (department, ethnic group, women, older workers, etc) might you have missed hearing from in your company, and how might you amplify this voice to create positive momentum for your business?
<--- Score

129. What was the last experiment you ran?
<--- Score

130. Do you feel that more should be done in the

video communication area?
<--- Score

131. What happens if you do not have enough funding?
<--- Score

132. What are you challenging?
<--- Score

133. Is maximizing video communication protection the same as minimizing video communication loss?
<--- Score

134. What knowledge, skills and characteristics mark a good video communication project manager?
<--- Score

135. Why not do video communication?
<--- Score

136. How do you transition from the baseline to the target?
<--- Score

137. What must you excel at?
<--- Score

138. Do you have the right capabilities and capacities?
<--- Score

139. What are internal and external video communication relations?
<--- Score

140. What role does communication play in the

success or failure of a video communication project?
<--- Score

141. Who do you think the world wants your organization to be?
<--- Score

142. Can you do all this work?
<--- Score

143. At what moment would you think; Will I get fired?
<--- Score

144. How do you accomplish your long range video communication goals?
<--- Score

145. If no one would ever find out about your accomplishments, how would you lead differently?
<--- Score

146. What relationships among video communication trends do you perceive?
<--- Score

147. How do you provide a safe environment -physically and emotionally?
<--- Score

148. Will it be accepted by users?
<--- Score

149. How do you keep the momentum going?
<--- Score

150. What did you miss in the interview for the worst

hire you ever made?
<--- Score

151. What is the craziest thing you can do?
<--- Score

152. Would you rather sell to knowledgeable and informed customers or to uninformed customers?
<--- Score

153. How long will it take to change?
<--- Score

154. Who do we want your customers to become?
<--- Score

155. In the past year, what have you done (or could you have done) to increase the accurate perception of your company/brand as ethical and honest?
<--- Score

156. If your customer were your grandmother, would you tell her to buy what you're selling?
<--- Score

157. What new services of functionality will be implemented next with video communication ?
<--- Score

158. How important is video communication to the user organizations mission?
<--- Score

159. What is an unauthorized commitment?
<--- Score

160. In a project to restructure video communication outcomes, which stakeholders would you involve?
<--- Score

161. In retrospect, of the projects that you pulled the plug on, what percent do you wish had been allowed to keep going, and what percent do you wish had ended earlier?
<--- Score

162. Who is responsible for ensuring appropriate resources (time, people and money) are allocated to video communication?
<--- Score

163. Who, on the executive team or the board, has spoken to a customer recently?
<--- Score

164. Marketing budgets are tighter, consumers are more skeptical, and social media has changed forever the way we talk about video communication, how do you gain traction?
<--- Score

165. Which functions and people interact with the supplier and or customer?
<--- Score

166. Is your basic point _____ or _____?
<--- Score

167. Who is responsible for errors?
<--- Score

168. What are specific video communication rules to follow?

<--- Score

169. Political -is anyone trying to undermine this project?

<--- Score

170. Who are four people whose careers you have enhanced?

<--- Score

171. If you find that you havent accomplished one of the goals for one of the steps of the video communication strategy, what will you do to fix it?

<--- Score

172. Who will be responsible for deciding whether video communication goes ahead or not after the initial investigations?

<--- Score

173. If you got fired and a new hire took your place, what would she do different?

<--- Score

174. How is implementation research currently incorporated into each of your goals?

<--- Score

175. Whom among your colleagues do you trust, and for what?

<--- Score

176. Is the video communication organization completing tasks effectively and efficiently?

<--- Score

177. If you do not follow, then how to lead?
<--- Score

178. Is there any existing video communication governance structure?
<--- Score

179. What is the estimated value of the project?
<--- Score

180. Will there be any necessary staff changes (redundancies or new hires)?
<--- Score

181. If you had to leave your organization for a year and the only communication you could have with employees/colleagues was a single paragraph, what would you write?
<--- Score

182. What is the purpose of video communication in relation to the mission?
<--- Score

183. How do you know if you are successful?
<--- Score

184. What are the business goals video communication is aiming to achieve?
<--- Score

185. How do you govern and fulfill your societal responsibilities?
<--- Score

186. What are the barriers to increased video communication production?
<--- Score

187. How do you ensure that implementations of video communication products are done in a way that ensures safety?
<--- Score

188. Who will manage the integration of tools?
<--- Score

189. What are the rules and assumptions your industry operates under? What if the opposite were true?
<--- Score

Add up total points for this section:
_ _ _ _ _ = Total points for this section

Divided by: _ _ _ _ _ _ (number of statements answered) = _ _ _ _ _ _
Average score for this section

Transfer your score to the video communication Index at the beginning of the Self-Assessment.

Video Communication and Managing Projects, Criteria for Project Managers:

1.0 Initiating Process Group: Video Communication

1. How well did the chosen processes fit the needs of the Video Communication project?

2. Information sharing?

3. Mitigate. what will you do to minimize the impact should the risk event occur?

4. Did the Video Communication project team have the right skills?

5. Are stakeholders properly informed about the status of the Video Communication project?

6. Have the stakeholders identified all individual requirements pertaining to business process?

7. Who is performing the work of the Video Communication project?

8. How should needs be met?

9. How to control and approve each phase?

10. How is each deliverable reviewed, verified, and validated?

11. What communication items need improvement?

12. Which of six sigmas dmaic phases focuses on the measurement of internal process that affect factors that are critical to quality?

13. How will you know you did it?

14. How well defined and documented were the Video Communication project management processes you chose to use?

15. Did the Video Communication project team have the right skills?

16. What are the pressing issues of the hour?

17. At which cmmi level are software processes documented, standardized, and integrated into a standard to-be practiced process for your organization?

18. Do you know all the stakeholders impacted by the Video Communication project and what needs are?

19. If action is called for, what form should it take?

20. Do you know the Video Communication projects goal, purpose and objectives?

1.1 Project Charter: Video Communication

21. What goes into your Video Communication project Charter?

22. Why Outsource?

23. Who ise input and support will this Video Communication project require?

24. Does the Video Communication project need to consider any special capacity or capability issues?

25. Environmental stewardship and sustainability considerations: what is the process that will be used to ensure compliance with the environmental stewardship policy?

26. Who are the stakeholders?

27. Why executive support?

28. What are the constraints?

29. Are there special technology requirements?

30. Are you building in-house ?

31. What metrics could you look at?

32. Who will take notes, document decisions?

33. When?

34. What changes can you make to improve?

35. Market – identify products market, including whether it is outside of the objective: what is the purpose of the program or Video Communication project?

36. What ideas do you have for initial tests of change (PDSA cycles)?

37. Is time of the essence?

38. Run it as as a startup?

39. What does it need to do?

1.2 Stakeholder Register: Video Communication

40. Who wants to talk about Security?

41. How should employers make voices heard?

42. How big is the gap?

43. Who is managing stakeholder engagement?

44. What are the major Video Communication project milestones requiring communications or providing communications opportunities?

45. How much influence do they have on the Video Communication project?

46. Is your organization ready for change?

47. How will reports be created?

48. What opportunities exist to provide communications?

49. What is the power of the stakeholder?

50. What & Why?

1.3 Stakeholder Analysis Matrix: Video Communication

51. Volumes, production, economies?

52. Who will be affected by the Video Communication project?

53. How do rules, behaviors affect stakes?

54. Are the required specifications for products or services changing?

55. Global influences?

56. What is accountability in relation to the Video Communication project?

57. Benefit to whom?

58. What is the range you need to look at?

59. New technologies, services, ideas?

60. Will the impacts be local, national or international?

61. What is the stakeholders name, what is function?

62. Contributions to policy and practice?

63. Political effects?

64. Supporters; who are the supporters?

65. Why is it important to identify them?

66. What unique or lowest-cost resources does the Video Communication project have access to?

67. Participatory approach: how will key stakeholders participate in the Video Communication project?

68. What is your organizations competitors doing?

69. What do you need to appraise?

70. Who is most dependent on the resources at stake?

2.0 Planning Process Group: Video Communication

71. The Video Communication project charter is created in which Video Communication project management process group?

72. Contingency planning. if a risk event occurs, what will you do?

73. What input will you be required to provide the Video Communication project team?

74. Did the program design/ implementation strategy adequately address the planning stage necessary to set up structures, hire staff etc.?

75. On which process should team members spend the most time?

76. How are the principles of aid effectiveness (ownership, alignment, management for development results and mutual responsibility) being applied in the Video Communication project?

77. In what way has the Video Communication project come up with innovative measures for problem-solving?

78. What is the difference between the early schedule and late schedule?

79. What is the NEXT thing to do?

80. Is the duration of the program sufficient to ensure a cycle that will Video Communication project the sustainability of the interventions?

81. How can you make your needs known?

82. How well did the chosen processes fit the needs of the Video Communication project?

83. Have operating capacities been created and/or reinforced in partners?

84. Why do it Video Communication projects fail?

85. Have more efficient (sensitive) and appropriate measures been adopted to respond to the political and socio-cultural problems identified?

86. You are creating your WBS and find that you keep decomposing tasks into smaller and smaller units. How can you tell when you are done?

87. How can you tell when you are done?

88. Why is it important to determine activity sequencing on Video Communication projects?

89. What is a Software Development Life Cycle (SDLC)?

90. Will the products created live up to the necessary quality?

2.1 Project Management Plan: Video Communication

91. Is mitigation authorized or recommended?

92. Does the selected plan protect privacy?

93. Who is the Video Communication project Manager?

94. What happened during the process that you found interesting?

95. When is the Video Communication project management plan created?

96. What would you do differently?

97. What are the known stakeholder requirements?

98. What are the training needs?

99. Are cost risk analysis methods applied to develop contingencies for the estimated total Video Communication project costs?

100. If the Video Communication project is complex or scope is specialized, do you have appropriate and/or qualified staff available to perform the tasks?

101. Who is the sponsor?

102. Is the budget realistic?

103. Is there anything you would now do differently on your Video Communication project based on past experience?

104. What is the business need?

105. Do the proposed changes from the Video Communication project include any significant risks to safety?

106. Are the existing and future without-plan conditions reasonable and appropriate?

107. Are calculations and results of analyzes essentially correct?

108. Are alternatives safe, functional, constructible, economical, reasonable and sustainable?

109. What did not work so well?

110. What are the deliverables?

2.2 Scope Management Plan: Video Communication

111. Does all Video Communication project documentation reside in a common repository for easy access?

112. When is corrective or preventative action required?

113. Is a pmo (Video Communication project management office) in place and provide oversight to the Video Communication project?

114. Has a capability assessment been conducted?

115. How are you planning to maintain the scope baseline and how will you manage scope changes?

116. Are written status reports provided on a designated frequent basis?

117. Does the resource management plan include a personnel development plan?

118. Can the Video Communication project team do several activities in parallel?

119. Is the assigned Video Communication project manager a PMP (Certified Video Communication project manager) and experienced?

120. Time estimation – how much time will be

needed?

121. Staffing Requirements?

122. Are you meeting with stake holders and team members?

123. Do all stakeholders know how to access this repository and where to find the Video Communication project documentation?

124. How do you know when you are finished?

125. Has the selected plan been formulated using cost effectiveness and incremental analysis techniques?

126. Are trade-offs between accepting the risk and mitigating the risk identified?

127. Is stakeholder involvement adequate?

128. Is an industry recognized mechanized support tool(s) being used for Video Communication project scheduling & tracking?

129. Does the Video Communication project have a Statement of Work?

130. Are decisions captured in a decisions log?

2.3 Requirements Management Plan: Video Communication

131. Is infrastructure setup part of your Video Communication project?

132. To see if a requirement statement is sufficiently well-defined, read it from the developers perspective. Mentally add the phrase, call me when youre done to the end of the requirement and see if that makes you nervous. In other words, would you need additional clarification from the author to understand the requirement well enough to design and implement it?

133. Did you provide clear and concise specifications?

134. Who is responsible for quantifying the Video Communication project requirements?

135. Have stakeholders been instructed in the Change Control process?

136. Which hardware or software, related to, or as outcome of the Video Communication project is new to your organization?

137. Will you perform a Requirements Risk assessment and develop a plan to deal with risks?

138. Is the change control process documented?

139. Will you use tracing to help understand the impact of a change in requirements?

140. What performance metrics will be used?

141. How knowledgeable is the team in the proposed application area?

142. Is there formal agreement on who has authority to request a change in requirements?

143. What are you counting on?

144. Will the contractors involved take full responsibility?

145. Who will approve the requirements (and if multiple approvers, in what order)?

146. Is stakeholder risk tolerance an important factor for the requirements process in this Video Communication project?

147. Will you have access to stakeholders when you need them?

148. How will bidders price evaluations be done, by deliverables, phases, or in a big bang?

149. How often will the reporting occur?

150. What cost metrics will be used?

2.4 Requirements Documentation: Video Communication

151. Who is involved?

152. How do you know when a Requirement is accurate enough?

153. Completeness. are all functions required by the customer included?

154. Can you check system requirements?

155. How does what is being described meet the business need?

156. Does your organization restrict technical alternatives?

157. Are there legal issues?

158. How will the proposed Video Communication project help?

159. Basic work/business process; high-level, what is being touched?

160. Can the requirement be changed without a large impact on other requirements?

161. What variations exist for a process?

162. Where are business rules being captured?

163. Verifiability. can the requirements be checked?

164. How can you document system requirements?

165. What marketing channels do you want to use: e-mail, letter or sms?

166. What kind of entity is a problem ?

167. What will be the integration problems?

168. What images does it conjure?

169. How much does requirements engineering cost?

170. What are the potential disadvantages/ advantages?

2.5 Requirements Traceability Matrix: Video Communication

171. Why use a WBS?

172. What percentage of Video Communication projects are producing traceability matrices between requirements and other work products?

173. Will you use a Requirements Traceability Matrix?

174. Do you have a clear understanding of all subcontracts in place?

175. What are the chronologies, contingencies, consequences, criteria?

176. How do you manage scope?

177. How small is small enough?

178. How will it affect the stakeholders personally in career?

179. Is there a requirements traceability process in place?

180. Describe the process for approving requirements so they can be added to the traceability matrix and Video Communication project work can be performed. Will the Video Communication project requirements become approved in writing?

181. Why do you manage scope?

182. What is the WBS?

2.6 Project Scope Statement: Video Communication

183. Is the change control process documented and on file?

184. Is there a baseline plan against which to measure progress?

185. Is the scope of your Video Communication project well defined?

186. Will the risk plan be updated on a regular and frequent basis?

187. Was planning completed before the Video Communication project was initiated?

188. Change management vs. change leadership - what is the difference?

189. Is there a process (test plans, inspections, reviews) defined for verifying outputs for each task?

190. Have the configuration management functions been assigned?

191. Why do you need to manage scope?

192. Is there a Quality Assurance Plan documented and filed?

193. Is there an information system for the Video

Communication project?

194. How will you verify the accuracy of the work of the Video Communication project, and what constitutes acceptance of the deliverables?

195. What is the most common tool for helping define the detail?

196. Risks?

197. Is the plan for your organization of the Video Communication project resources adequate?

198. What process would you recommend for creating the Video Communication project scope statement?

199. Once its defined, what is the stability of the Video Communication project scope?

200. Will tasks be marked complete only after QA has been successfully completed?

201. Any new risks introduced or old risks impacted. Are there issues that could affect the existing requirements for the result, service, or product if the scope changes?

202. Elements of scope management that deal with concept development ?

2.7 Assumption and Constraint Log: Video Communication

203. Is the amount of effort justified by the anticipated value of forming a new process?

204. Do documented requirements exist for all critical components and areas, including technical, business, interfaces, performance, security and conversion requirements?

205. Is staff trained on the software technologies that are being used on the Video Communication project?

206. What weaknesses do you have?

207. Is this model reasonable?

208. Have you eliminated all duplicative tasks or manual efforts, where appropriate?

209. What is positive about the current process?

210. Are formal code reviews conducted?

211. How can constraints be violated?

212. Are requirements management tracking tools and procedures in place?

213. Are there processes in place to ensure that all the terms and code concepts have been documented consistently?

214. Are there procedures in place to effectively manage interdependencies with other Video Communication projects / systems?

215. What worked well?

216. Does the plan conform to standards?

217. Are there ways to reduce the time it takes to get something approved?

218. How are new requirements or changes to requirements identified?

219. Has a Video Communication project Communications Plan been developed?

220. What if failure during recovery?

221. Does a specific action and/or state that is known to violate security policy occur?

222. Is there a Steering Committee in place?

2.8 Work Breakdown Structure: Video Communication

223. What is the probability of completing the Video Communication project in less that xx days?

224. Why would you develop a Work Breakdown Structure?

225. When does it have to be done?

226. How far down?

227. How much detail?

228. What is the probability that the Video Communication project duration will exceed xx weeks?

229. When would you develop a Work Breakdown Structure?

230. Who has to do it?

231. How will you and your Video Communication project team define the Video Communication projects scope and work breakdown structure?

232. Why is it useful?

233. Do you need another level?

234. Is it still viable?

235. When do you stop?

236. Is the work breakdown structure (wbs) defined and is the scope of the Video Communication project clear with assigned deliverable owners?

237. Can you make it?

238. How big is a work-package?

239. Where does it take place?

2.9 WBS Dictionary: Video Communication

240. Wbs elements contractually specified for reporting of status to you (lowest level only)?

241. Is the work done on a work package level as described in the WBS dictionary?

242. Are overhead cost budgets established for each organization which has authority to incur overhead costs?

243. Is subcontracted work defined and identified to the appropriate subcontractor within the proper WBS element?

244. Budgets assigned to major functional organizations?

245. Are management actions taken to reduce indirect costs when there are significant adverse variances?

246. Are the procedures for identifying indirect costs to incurring organizations, indirect cost pools, and allocating the costs from the pools to the contracts formally documented?

247. Are estimates of costs at completion utilized in determining contract funding requirements and reporting them?

248. Time-phased control account budgets?

249. Are data elements summarized through the functional organizational structure for progressively higher levels of management?

250. Are indirect costs accumulated for comparison with the corresponding budgets?

251. Are Video Communication projected overhead costs in each pool and the associated direct costs used as the basis for establishing interim rates for allocating overhead to contracts?

252. The total budget for the contract (including estimates for authorized and unpriced work)?

253. Are the variances between budgeted and actual indirect costs identified and analyzed at the level of assigned responsibility for control (indirect pool, department, etc.)?

254. Are the requirements for all items of overhead established by rational, traceable processes?

255. Does the contractors system provide for the determination of cost variances attributable to the excess usage of material?

256. Are overhead budgets and costs being handled according to the disclosure statement when applicable, or otherwise properly classified (for example, engineering overhead, IR&D)?

257. Does the contractors system provide unit or lot costs when applicable?

258. Do the lines of authority for incurring indirect costs correspond to the lines of responsibility for management control of the same components of costs?

259. Are retroactive changes to budgets for completed work specifically prohibited in an established procedure, and is this procedure adhered to?

2.10 Schedule Management Plan: Video Communication

260. Are adequate resources provided for the quality assurance function?

261. What will be the format of the schedule model?

262. Are Video Communication project leaders committed to this Video Communication project full time?

263. Does the detailed work plan match the complexity of tasks with the capabilities of personnel?

264. How do you manage time?

265. Is Video Communication project status reviewed with the steering and executive teams at appropriate intervals?

266. Are Video Communication project team members committed fulltime?

267. Has the Video Communication project manager been identified?

268. Is the ims used by all levels of management for Video Communication project implementation and control?

269. Sensitivity analysis?

270. Is there a procedure for management, control and release of schedule margin?

271. How are Video Communication projects different from operations?

272. Is the quality assurance team identified?

273. Were the budget estimates reasonable?

274. Can additional resources be added to subsequent tasks to reduce the durations of the already stated tasks?

275. Are metrics used to evaluate and manage Vendors?

276. Have the key elements of a coherent Video Communication project management strategy been established?

277. Have all unresolved risks been documented?

2.11 Activity List: Video Communication

278. What did not go as well?

279. What went wrong?

280. What is the probability the Video Communication project can be completed in xx weeks?

281. Who will perform the work?

282. How difficult will it be to do specific activities on this Video Communication project?

283. When do the individual activities need to start and finish?

284. How can the Video Communication project be displayed graphically to better visualize the activities?

285. In what sequence?

286. Should you include sub-activities?

287. What went right?

288. What is the LF and LS for each activity?

289. Where will it be performed?

290. What is your organizations history in doing similar activities?

291. How will it be performed?

292. What are the critical bottleneck activities?

293. Are the required resources available or need to be acquired?

294. The wbs is developed as part of a joint planning session. and how do you know that youhave done this right?

295. What will be performed?

296. Is there anything planned that does not need to be here?

2.12 Activity Attributes: Video Communication

297. Is there a trend during the year?

298. How much activity detail is required?

299. Activity: fair or not fair?

300. Has management defined a definite timeframe for the turnaround or Video Communication project window?

301. Where else does it apply?

302. How difficult will it be to complete specific activities on this Video Communication project?

303. Resource is assigned to?

304. How else could the items be grouped?

305. What conclusions/generalizations can you draw from this?

306. Are the required resources available?

307. Does your organization of the data change its meaning?

308. Resources to accomplish the work?

309. Do you feel very comfortable with your

prediction?

310. What is missing?

311. Have constraints been applied to the start and finish milestones for the phases?

312. Can more resources be added?

313. What activity do you think you should spend the most time on?

314. How difficult will it be to do specific activities on this Video Communication project?

2.13 Milestone List: Video Communication

315. Information and research?

316. Do you foresee any technical risks or developmental challenges?

317. When will the Video Communication project be complete?

318. What is the market for your technology, product or service?

319. How will the milestone be verified?

320. How late can each activity be finished and started?

321. What date will the task finish?

322. Sustaining internal capabilities?

323. Describe the industry you are in and the market growth opportunities. What is the market for your technology, product or service?

324. Sustainable financial backing?

325. Loss of key staff?

326. Gaps in capabilities?

327. Marketing - reach, distribution, awareness?

328. Describe your organizations strengths and core competencies. What factors will make your organization succeed?

329. How late can the activity start?

330. Level of the Innovation?

331. Vital contracts and partners?

332. Can you derive how soon can the whole Video Communication project finish?

2.14 Network Diagram: Video Communication

333. What are the tools?

334. What job or jobs could run concurrently?

335. What is the probability of completing the Video Communication project in less that xx days?

336. Will crashing x weeks return more in benefits than it costs?

337. What is the lowest cost to complete this Video Communication project in xx weeks?

338. Why must you schedule milestones, such as reviews, throughout the Video Communication project?

339. Exercise: what is the probability that the Video Communication project duration will exceed xx weeks?

340. Are you on time?

341. If a current contract exists, can you provide the vendor name, contract start, and contract expiration date?

342. Which type of network diagram allows you to depict four types of dependencies?

343. What are the Key Success Factors?

344. What job or jobs follow it?

345. What activity must be completed immediately before this activity can start?

346. Where do schedules come from?

347. What activities must occur simultaneously with this activity?

348. Can you calculate the confidence level?

349. How confident can you be in your milestone dates and the delivery date?

2.15 Activity Resource Requirements: Video Communication

350. Anything else?

351. How many signatures do you require on a check and does this match what is in your policy and procedures?

352. When does monitoring begin?

353. What is the Work Plan Standard?

354. Why do you do that?

355. Are there unresolved issues that need to be addressed?

356. Other support in specific areas?

357. Organizational Applicability?

358. Do you use tools like decomposition and rolling-wave planning to produce the activity list and other outputs?

359. How do you handle petty cash?

360. What are constraints that you might find during the Human Resource Planning process?

361. Time for overtime?

362. Which logical relationship does the PDM use most often?

2.16 Resource Breakdown Structure: Video Communication

363. Which resources should be in the resource pool?

364. How difficult will it be to do specific activities on this Video Communication project?

365. Any changes from stakeholders?

366. Why do you do it?

367. What is the primary purpose of the human resource plan?

368. Why time management?

369. What defines a successful Video Communication project?

370. What is Video Communication project communication management?

371. What is the number one predictor of a groups productivity?

372. When do they need the information?

373. What is the purpose of assigning and documenting responsibility?

374. Who will be used as a Video Communication project team member?

375. Who is allowed to perform which functions?

376. Why is this important?

377. Changes based on input from stakeholders?

378. What are the requirements for resource data?

379. What is the difference between % Complete and % work?

380. Who will use the system?

2.17 Activity Duration Estimates: Video Communication

381. What is done after activity duration estimation?

382. What are crucial elements of successful Video Communication project plan execution?

383. How can software assist in procuring goods and services?

384. What is pmp certification, and why do you think the number of people earning it has grown so much in the past ten years?

385. Are resource rates available to calculate Video Communication project costs?

386. List five reasons why organizations outsource. Why is there a growing trend in outsourcing, especially in the government?

387. Consider the common sources of risk on information technology Video Communication projects and suggestions for managing them. Which suggestions do you find most useful?

388. Which includes asking team members about the time estimates for activities and reaching agreement on the calendar date for each activity?

389. What do corresponding sources say about Video Communication project management?

390. What are the Video Communication project management deliverables of each process group?

391. How do theories relate to Video Communication project management?

392. Do your results resemble a normal distribution?

393. How many different communications channels does a Video Communication project team with six people have?

394. What are the nine areas of expertise?

395. Consider the history of modern quality management. How have experts such as Deming, Juran, Crosby, and Taguchi affected the quality movement and todays use of Six Sigma?

396. What is the duration of the critical path for this Video Communication project?

397. Which best describes how this affects the Video Communication project?

398. Research risk management software. Are many products available?

2.18 Duration Estimating Worksheet: Video Communication

399. How can the Video Communication project be displayed graphically to better visualize the activities?

400. Do any colleagues have experience with your organization and/or RFPs?

401. For other activities, how much delay can be tolerated?

402. What is the total time required to complete the Video Communication project if no delays occur?

403. Can the Video Communication project be constructed as planned?

404. Value pocket identification & quantification what are value pockets?

405. Does the Video Communication project provide innovative ways for stakeholders to overcome obstacles or deliver better outcomes?

406. What is next?

407. What is cost and Video Communication project cost management?

408. Is the Video Communication project responsive to community need?

409. Done before proceeding with this activity or what can be done concurrently?

410. Why estimate time and cost?

411. What is an Average Video Communication project?

412. Is this operation cost effective?

413. What is your role?

414. Small or large Video Communication project?

415. What questions do you have?

2.19 Project Schedule: Video Communication

416. It allows the Video Communication project to be delivered on schedule. How Do you Use Schedules?

417. Are activities connected because logic dictates the order in which others occur?

418. Month Video Communication project take?

419. Why do you need to manage Video Communication project Risk?

420. Are key risk mitigation strategies added to the Video Communication project schedule?

421. How detailed should a Video Communication project get?

422. What is risk?

423. How many levels?

424. What is the purpose of a Video Communication project schedule?

425. Did the Video Communication project come in on schedule?

426. To what degree is do you feel the entire team was committed to the Video Communication project schedule?

427. How effectively were issues able to be resolved without impacting the Video Communication project Schedule or Budget?

428. Are quality inspections and review activities listed in the Video Communication project schedule(s)?

429. Is there a Schedule Management Plan that establishes the criteria and activities for developing, monitoring and controlling the Video Communication project schedule?

430. Meet requirements?

431. Are procedures defined by which the Video Communication project schedule may be changed?

432. Does the condition or event threaten the Video Communication projects objectives in any ways?

433. How do you use schedules?

2.20 Cost Management Plan: Video Communication

434. Were Video Communication project team members involved in detailed estimating and scheduling?

435. What strengths do you have?

436. Have the procedures for identifying budget variances been followed?

437. Outside experts?

438. Is there a set of procedures defining the scope, procedures, and deliverables defining quality control?

439. Is your organization certified as a broker of the products/supplies?

440. Responsibilities – what is the split of responsibilities between the owner and contractors?

441. Has a resource management plan been created?

442. Is there a formal set of procedures supporting Stakeholder Management?

443. Are tasks tracked by hours?

444. Has the scope management document been updated and distributed to help prevent scope creep?

445. Is it possible to track all classes of Video Communication project work (e.g. scheduled, unscheduled, defect repair, etc.)?

446. Are all payments made according to the contract(s)?

447. Does all Video Communication project documentation reside in a common repository for easy access?

448. Forecasts – how will the cost to complete the Video Communication project be forecast?

449. The definition of the Video Communication project scope what needs to be accomplished?

2.21 Activity Cost Estimates: Video Communication

450. Are cost subtotals needed?

451. How Award?

452. Are data needed on characteristics of care?

453. Which contract type places the most risk on the seller?

454. Were the costs or charges reasonable?

455. What skill level is required to do the job?

456. Does the activity rely on a common set of tools to carry it out?

457. How do you change activities?

458. What were things that you need to improve?

459. Can you change your activities?

460. What happens if you cannot produce the documentation for the single audit?

461. Based on your Video Communication project communication management plan, what worked well?

462. Where can you get activity reports?

463. What is your organizations history in doing similar tasks?

464. What makes a good activity description?

465. What is the activity inventory?

466. Were escalated issues resolved promptly?

467. What areas does the group agree are the biggest success on the Video Communication project?

468. What is a Video Communication project Management Plan?

469. Vac -variance at completion, how much over/ under budget do you expect to be?

2.22 Cost Estimating Worksheet: Video Communication

470. Can a trend be established from historical performance data on the selected measure and are the criteria for using trend analysis or forecasting methods met?

471. Is it feasible to establish a control group arrangement?

472. What will others want?

473. What can be included?

474. What info is needed?

475. Ask: are others positioned to know, are others credible, and will others cooperate?

476. Who is best positioned to know and assist in identifying corresponding factors?

477. Is the Video Communication project responsive to community need?

478. Does the Video Communication project provide innovative ways for stakeholders to overcome obstacles or deliver better outcomes?

479. What is the estimated labor cost today based upon this information?

480. What is the purpose of estimating?

481. What happens to any remaining funds not used?

482. What additional Video Communication project(s) could be initiated as a result of this Video Communication project?

483. How will the results be shared and to whom?

484. What costs are to be estimated?

485. Will the Video Communication project collaborate with the local community and leverage resources?

486. Identify the timeframe necessary to monitor progress and collect data to determine how the selected measure has changed?

2.23 Cost Baseline: Video Communication

487. Has the Video Communication projected annual cost to operate and maintain the product(s) or service(s) been approved and funded?

488. Impact to environment?

489. Are there contingencies or conditions related to the acceptance?

490. Have all approved changes to the cost baseline been identified and impact on the Video Communication project documented?

491. Does a process exist for establishing a cost baseline to measure Video Communication project performance?

492. What is the consequence?

493. Are you meeting with your team regularly?

494. Has the documentation relating to operation and maintenance of the product(s) or service(s) been delivered to, and accepted by, operations management?

495. Video Communication project goals -should others be reconsidered?

496. Why do you manage cost?

497. What deliverables come first?

498. How concrete were original objectives?

499. For what purpose ?

500. If you sold 10x widgets on a day, what would the affect on profits be?

501. When should cost estimates be developed?

502. Will the Video Communication project fail if the change request is not executed?

503. Has the appropriate access to relevant data and analysis capability been granted?

504. Has the actual cost of the Video Communication project (or Video Communication project phase) been tallied and compared to the approved budget?

2.24 Quality Management Plan: Video Communication

505. Can you perform this task or activity in a more effective manner?

506. Meet how often?

507. Have all necessary approvals been obtained?

508. Would impacts defined serve as impediments?

509. Do trained quality assurance auditors conduct the audits as defined in the Quality Management Plan and scheduled by the Video Communication project manager?

510. How are corresponding standards measured?

511. How are calibration records kept?

512. Contradictory information between document sections?

513. What else should you do now?

514. Why quality management?

515. What field records are generated?

516. How does your organization decide what to measure?

517. What does it do for you (or to me)?

518. How is staff trained on the recording of field notes?

519. Have all involved stakeholders and work groups committed to the Video Communication project?

520. Are there nonconformance issues?

521. Sampling part of task?

522. Diagrams and tables to account for complex concepts and increase overall readability?

523. How does your organization use comparative data and information to improve organizational performance?

2.25 Quality Metrics: Video Communication

524. There are many reasons to shore up quality-related metrics, and what metrics are important?

525. Filter visualizations of interest?

526. Subjective quality component: customer satisfaction, how do you measure it?

527. Are quality metrics defined?

528. Has risk analysis been adequately reviewed?

529. What can manufacturing professionals do to ensure quality is seen as an integral part of the entire product lifecycle?

530. Are there any open risk issues?

531. How do you know if everyone is trying to improve the right things?

532. How is it being measured?

533. What forces exist that would cause them to change?

534. Do the operators focus on determining; is there anything you need to worry about?

535. Have risk areas been identified?

536. Does risk analysis documentation meet standards?

537. Is quality culture a competitive advantage?

538. What level of statistical confidence do you use?

539. Where is quality now?

540. Have alternatives been defined in the event that failure occurs?

541. What is the timeline to meet your goal?

542. What happens if you get an abnormal result?

543. What metrics are important and most beneficial to measure?

2.26 Process Improvement Plan: Video Communication

544. How do you measure?

545. What actions are needed to address the problems and achieve the goals?

546. Modeling current processes is great, and will you ever see a return on that investment?

547. Are there forms and procedures to collect and record the data?

548. Management commitment at all levels?

549. Are you making progress on the goals?

550. Does explicit definition of the measures exist?

551. What lessons have you learned so far?

552. What is the test-cycle concept?

553. Are you making progress on your improvement plan?

554. If a process improvement framework is being used, which elements will help the problems and goals listed?

555. Have the supporting tools been developed or acquired?

556. What personnel are the champions for the initiative?

557. Are you making progress on the improvement framework?

558. Does your process ensure quality?

559. What makes people good SPI coaches?

560. What personnel are the coaches for your initiative?

561. The motive is determined by asking, Why do you want to achieve this goal?

562. What is quality and how will you ensure it?

2.27 Responsibility Assignment Matrix: Video Communication

563. Who is going to do that work?

564. Wbs elements contractually specified for reporting of status (lowest level only)?

565. Are records maintained to show how undistributed budgets are controlled?

566. Are the bases and rates for allocating costs from each indirect pool consistently applied?

567. The already stated responsible for the establishment of budgets and assignment of resources for overhead performance?

568. Are detailed work packages planned as far in advance as practicable?

569. Does the accounting system provide a basis for auditing records of direct costs chargeable to the contract?

570. Authorization to proceed with all authorized work?

571. What are the assumptions?

572. Identify potential or actual budget-based and time-based schedule variances?

573. Is the entire contract planned in time-phased control accounts to the extent practicable?

574. The anticipated business volume?

575. When performing is split among two or more roles, is the work clearly defined so that the efforts are coordinated and the communication is clear?

576. Cwbs elements to be subcontracted, with identification of subcontractors?

577. Evaluate the performance of operating organizations?

578. Are all authorized tasks assigned to identified organizational elements?

579. No rs: if a task has no one listed as responsible, who is getting the job done?

580. What materials and procurements needed?

2.28 Roles and Responsibilities: Video Communication

581. Once the responsibilities are defined for the Video Communication project, have the deliverables, roles and responsibilities been clearly communicated to every participant?

582. Who: who is involved?

583. What areas would you highlight for changes or improvements?

584. What expectations were NOT met?

585. Concern: where are you limited or have no authority, where you can not influence?

586. Authority: what areas/Video Communication projects in your work do you have the authority to decide upon and act on the already stated decisions?

587. Are Video Communication project team roles and responsibilities identified and documented?

588. What areas of supervision are challenging for you?

589. Influence: what areas of organizational decision making are you able to influence when you do not have authority to make the final decision?

590. What expectations were met?

591. What is working well within your organizations performance management system?

592. Once the responsibilities are defined for the Video Communication project, have the deliverables, roles and responsibilities been clearly communicated to every participant?

593. What is working well?

594. What specific behaviors did you observe?

595. Was the expectation clearly communicated?

596. What should you highlight for improvement?

597. To decide whether to use a quality measurement, ask how will you know when it is achieved?

598. Implementation of actions: Who are the responsible units?

2.29 Human Resource Management Plan: Video Communication

599. Is your organization primarily focused on a specific industry?

600. Is the communication plan being followed?

601. Is Video Communication project status reviewed with the steering and executive teams at appropriate intervals?

602. Is it possible to track all classes of Video Communication project work (e.g. scheduled, un-scheduled, defect repair, etc.)?

603. Is there a requirements change management processes in place?

604. Is there an on-going process in place to monitor Video Communication project risks?

605. Has your organization readiness assessment been conducted?

606. Have activity relationships and interdependencies within tasks been adequately identified?

607. Are Video Communication project team members committed fulltime?

608. Pareto diagrams, statistical sampling, flow

charting or trend analysis used quality monitoring?

609. Are changes in scope (deliverable commitments) agreed to by all affected groups & individuals?

610. Who are the people that make up your organization and whom create the success that your organization enjoys as a whole?

611. Identify who is needed on the core Video Communication project team to complete Video Communication project deliverables and achieve its goals and objectives. What skills, knowledge and experiences are required?

612. What are the Staffing Requirements?

613. Are the Video Communication project plans updated on a frequent basis?

614. What areas does the group agree are the biggest success on the Video Communication project?

615. Are key risk mitigation strategies added to the Video Communication project schedule?

616. What skills, knowledge and experiences are required?

617. Were sponsors and decision makers available when needed outside regularly scheduled meetings?

2.30 Communications Management Plan: Video Communication

618. Who is the stakeholder?

619. Who have you worked with in past, similar initiatives?

620. Are stakeholders internal or external?

621. Are there common objectives between the team and the stakeholder?

622. Which stakeholders are thought leaders, influences, or early adopters?

623. Who needs to know and how much?

624. Conflict resolution -which method when?

625. Are others part of the communications management plan?

626. Do you have members of your team responsible for certain stakeholders?

627. Do you feel more overwhelmed by stakeholders?

628. Why manage stakeholders?

629. Who to share with?

630. What is the stakeholders level of authority?

631. Is there an important stakeholder who is actively opposed and will not receive messages?

632. Timing: when do the effects of the communication take place?

633. Will messages be directly related to the release strategy or phases of the Video Communication project?

634. Are others needed?

635. What data is going to be required?

636. Why is stakeholder engagement important?

637. Do you then often overlook a key stakeholder or stakeholder group?

2.31 Risk Management Plan: Video Communication

638. Is the customer willing to commit significant time to the requirements gathering process?

639. Can the risk be avoided by choosing a different alternative?

640. What should be done with non-critical risks?

641. What can go wrong?

642. Risk documentation: what reporting formats and processes will be used for risk management activities?

643. For software; are compilers and code generators available and suitable for the product to be built?

644. Are there new risks that mitigation strategies might introduce?

645. Why do you need to manage Video Communication project Risk?

646. Are the reports useful and easy to read?

647. How much risk protection can you afford?

648. Are you on schedule?

649. Do end-users have realistic expectations?

650. What are the cost, schedule and resource impacts of avoiding the risk?

651. How is the audit profession changing?

652. Is security a central objective?

653. Who should be notified of the occurrence of each of the indicators?

654. Risks should be identified during which phase of Video Communication project management life cycle?

655. Is the customer willing to establish rapid communication links with the developer?

656. Have staff received necessary training?

657. Are requirements fully understood by the software engineering team and customers?

2.32 Risk Register: Video Communication

658. Market risk -will the new service or product be useful to your organization or marketable to others?

659. How could corresponding Risk affect the Video Communication project in terms of cost and schedule?

660. Risk categories: what are the main categories of risks that should be addressed on this Video Communication project?

661. People risk -are people with appropriate skills available to help complete the Video Communication project?

662. What further options might be available for responding to the risk?

663. Schedule impact/severity estimated range (workdays) assume the event happens, what is the potential impact?

664. Cost/benefit – how much will the proposed mitigations cost and how does this cost compare with the potential cost of the risk event/situation should it occur?

665. What may happen or not go according to plan?

666. Risk probability and impact: how will the

probabilities and impacts of risk items be assessed?

667. Are implemented controls working as others should?

668. Manageability – have mitigations to the risk been identified?

669. What should you do when?

670. Which key risks have ineffective responses or outstanding improvement actions?

671. What is the appropriate level of risk management for this Video Communication project?

672. Are there any gaps in the evidence?

673. Contingency actions - planned actions to reduce the immediate seriousness of the risk when it does occur. What should you do when?

674. Severity Prediction?

675. What can be done about it?

2.33 Probability and Impact Assessment: Video Communication

676. When and how will the recent breakthroughs in basic research lead to commercial products?

677. What is the likely future demand of the customer?

678. How solid is the Video Communication projection of competitive reaction?

679. Who has experience with this?

680. Can it be enlarged by drawing people from other areas of your organization?

681. Are staff committed for the duration of the Video Communication project?

682. Is there additional information that would make you more confident about your analysis?

683. What will be cost of redeployment of personnel?

684. What are your data sources?

685. Risk urgency assessment -which of your risks could occur soon, or require a longer planning time?

686. What should be the level of coordination?

687. Do the requirements require the creation of new

algorithms?

688. What is the likelihood of a breakthrough?

689. Risk may be made during which step of risk management?

690. How is the risk management process used in practice?

691. Are some people working on multiple Video Communication projects?

692. What are its business ethics?

693. What is the past performance of the Video Communication project manager?

2.34 Probability and Impact Matrix: Video Communication

694. Has the need for the Video Communication project been properly established?

695. What are ways to measure and evaluate risks?

696. Is the present organizational structure for handling the Video Communication project sufficient?

697. What are the channels available for distribution to the customer?

698. How would you suggest monitoring for risk transition indicators?

699. How solid are the price-volume Video Communication projections?

700. Mandated delivery date?

701. What kind of preparation would be required to do this?

702. Mandated specific features?

703. Are the risk data complete?

704. Which role do you have in the Video Communication project?

705. How should you structure risks?

706. What should be the level of difficulty in handling the technology?

707. If you can not fix it, how do you do it differently?

708. Have top software and customer managers formally committed to support the Video Communication project?

709. Is there any sign of biased ranking?

710. Does the customer have a solid idea of what is required?

2.35 Risk Data Sheet: Video Communication

711. What was measured?

712. What are you here for (Mission)?

713. Will revised controls lead to tolerable risk levels?

714. What are the main opportunities available to you that you should grab while you can?

715. Is the data sufficiently specified in terms of the type of failure being analyzed, and its frequency or probability?

716. Whom do you serve (customers)?

717. Potential for recurrence?

718. What is the likelihood of it happening?

719. What will be the consequences if the risk happens?

720. How reliable is the data source?

721. What are the main threats to your existence?

722. What do you know?

723. What can you do?

724. How can hazards be reduced?

725. Who has a vested interest in how you perform as your organization (our stakeholders)?

726. Has a sensitivity analysis been carried out?

727. What are you trying to achieve (Objectives)?

728. What were the Causes that contributed?

729. What are your core values?

2.36 Procurement Management Plan: Video Communication

730. Specific - is the objective clear in terms of what, how, when, and where the situation will be changed?

731. What are you trying to accomplish?

732. Has a quality assurance plan been developed for the Video Communication project?

733. Are mitigation strategies identified?

734. How will you coordinate Procurement with aspects of the Video Communication project?

735. Are parking lot items captured?

736. Are meeting objectives identified for each meeting?

737. Financial capacity; does the seller have, or can the seller reasonably be expected to obtain, the financial resources needed?

738. What were things that you did well, and could improve, and how?

739. How long will it take for the purchase cost to be the same as the lease cost?

740. If independent estimates will be needed as evaluation criteria, who will prepare them and when?

741. Is the Video Communication project sponsor clearly communicating the business case or rationale for why this Video Communication project is needed?

742. Are assumptions being identified, recorded, analyzed, qualified and closed?

743. What areas are overlooked on this Video Communication project?

2.37 Source Selection Criteria: Video Communication

744. Is there collaboration among your evaluators?

745. Are responses to considerations adequate?

746. How can the methods of publicizing the buy be tailored to yield more effective price competition?

747. Is a letter of commitment from each proposed team member and key subcontractor included?

748. When must you conduct a debriefing?

749. How should the preproposal conference be conducted?

750. How are oral presentations documented?

751. What is the last item a Video Communication project manager must do to finalize Video Communication project close-out?

752. How should oral presentations be prepared for?

753. How do you manage procurement?

754. How do you encourage efficiency and consistency?

755. Are resultant proposal revisions allowed?

756. What can not be disclosed?

757. Is experience evaluated?

758. Who should attend debriefings?

759. What should a Draft Request for Proposal (DRFP) include?

760. Who is entitled to a debriefing?

761. What documentation is needed for a tradeoff decision?

762. What is the basis of an estimate and what assumptions were made?

2.38 Stakeholder Management Plan: Video Communication

763. After observing execution of process, is it in compliance with the documented Plan?

764. What are the advantages and disadvantages of using external contracted resources?

765. Which impacts could serve as impediments?

766. Are there processes in place to ensure internal consistency between the source code components?

767. What has to be purchased?

768. What is the drawback in using qualitative Video Communication project selection techniques?

769. What records are required (eg purchase orders, agreements)?

770. Are there standards for code development?

771. Does this include subcontracted development?

772. Are the appropriate IT resources adequate to meet planned commitments?

773. Have Video Communication project management standards and procedures been identified / established and documented?

774. How much information should be collected?

775. Have reserves been created to address risks?

776. What other teams / processes would be impacted by changes to the current process, and how?

777. Is documentation created for communication with the suppliers and vendors?

2.39 Change Management Plan: Video Communication

778. Where will the funds come from?

779. What relationships will change?

780. How far reaching in your organization is the change?

781. How frequently should you repeat the message?

782. What policies and procedures need to be changed?

783. Who will be the change levers?

784. Have the approved procedures and policies been published?

785. Who might present the most resistance?

786. How much change management is needed?

787. Who will fund the training?

788. Has the training co-ordinator been provided with the training details and put in place the necessary arrangements?

789. What are the responsibilities assigned to each role?

790. Who might be able to help you the most?

791. Will the readiness criteria be met prior to the training roll out?

792. What tasks are needed?

793. What risks may occur upfront?

794. Will a different work structure focus people on what is important?

795. What processes are in place to manage knowledge about the Video Communication project?

796. Has this been negotiated with the customer and sponsor?

797. Who should be involved in developing a change management strategy?

3.0 Executing Process Group: Video Communication

798. Is the schedule for the set products being met?

799. How do you measure difficulty?

800. What business situation is being addressed?

801. What are the critical steps involved with strategy mapping?

802. Measurable - are the targets measurable?

803. What good practices or successful experiences or transferable examples have been identified?

804. How do you control progress of your Video Communication project?

805. How can you use Microsoft Video Communication project and Excel to assist in Video Communication project risk management?

806. What type of people would you want on your team?

807. How will professionals learn what is expected from them what the deliverables are?

808. Based on your Video Communication project communication management plan, what worked well?

809. Would you rate yourself as being risk-averse, risk-neutral, or risk-seeking?

810. How well did the chosen processes fit the needs of the Video Communication project?

811. What were things that you did very well and want to do the same again on the next Video Communication project?

812. What will you do to minimize the impact should a risk event occur?

813. What areas does the group agree are the biggest success on the Video Communication project?

814. It under budget or over budget?

815. Are escalated issues resolved promptly?

3.1 Team Member Status Report: Video Communication

816. What is to be done?

817. Are the products of your organizations Video Communication projects meeting customers objectives?

818. How much risk is involved?

819. Are the attitudes of staff regarding Video Communication project work improving?

820. Does your organization have the means (staff, money, contract, etc.) to produce or to acquire the product, good, or service?

821. Do you have an Enterprise Video Communication project Management Office (EPMO)?

822. Are your organizations Video Communication projects more successful over time?

823. Will the staff do training or is that done by a third party?

824. Does the product, good, or service already exist within your organization?

825. Does every department have to have a Video Communication project Manager on staff?

826. The problem with Reward & Recognition Programs is that the truly deserving people all too often get left out. How can you make it practical?

827. What specific interest groups do you have in place?

828. Is there evidence that staff is taking a more professional approach toward management of your organizations Video Communication projects?

829. How will resource planning be done?

830. Why is it to be done?

831. How does this product, good, or service meet the needs of the Video Communication project and your organization as a whole?

832. How it is to be done?

833. When a teams productivity and success depend on collaboration and the efficient flow of information, what generally fails them?

834. How can you make it practical?

3.2 Change Request: Video Communication

835. Has the change been highlighted and documented in the CSCI?

836. When to submit a change request?

837. Who is responsible to authorize changes?

838. How are changes graded and who is responsible for the rating?

839. What must be taken into consideration when introducing change control programs?

840. Who can suggest changes?

841. Who is responsible for the implementation and monitoring of all measures?

842. What are the Impacts to your organization?

843. Why were your requested changes rejected or not made?

844. Who needs to approve change requests?

845. How shall the implementation of changes be recorded?

846. Screen shots or attachments included in a Change Request?

847. How does your organization control changes before and after software is released to a customer?

848. What are the basic mechanics of the Change Advisory Board (CAB)?

849. What is the change request log?

850. Will there be a change request form in use?

851. Why do you want to have a change control system?

852. How many lines of code must be changed to implement the change?

853. Has your address changed?

854. How to get changes (code) out in a timely manner?

3.3 Change Log: Video Communication

855. When was the request submitted?

856. Do the described changes impact on the integrity or security of the system?

857. When was the request approved?

858. Is this a mandatory replacement?

859. Is the change request within Video Communication project scope?

860. Is the requested change request a result of changes in other Video Communication project(s)?

861. Is the submitted change a new change or a modification of a previously approved change?

862. Does the suggested change request represent a desired enhancement to the products functionality?

863. Is the change backward compatible without limitations?

864. Will the Video Communication project fail if the change request is not executed?

865. How does this relate to the standards developed for specific business processes?

866. Does the suggested change request seem to represent a necessary enhancement to the product?

867. Who initiated the change request?

868. Where do changes come from?

869. How does this change affect scope?

870. How does this change affect the timeline of the schedule?

871. Is the change request open, closed or pending?

872. Should a more thorough impact analysis be conducted?

3.4 Decision Log: Video Communication

873. Meeting purpose; why does this team meet?

874. How do you define success?

875. How consolidated and comprehensive a story can you tell by capturing currently available incident data in a central location and through a log of key decisions during an incident?

876. What alternatives/risks were considered?

877. How does an increasing emphasis on cost containment influence the strategies and tactics used?

878. Which variables make a critical difference?

879. Is your opponent open to a non-traditional workflow, or will it likely challenge anything you do?

880. How does provision of information, both in terms of content and presentation, influence acceptance of alternative strategies?

881. At what point in time does loss become unacceptable?

882. Does anything need to be adjusted?

883. What is your overall strategy for quality control /

quality assurance procedures?

884. Is everything working as expected?

885. Adversarial environment. is your opponent open to a non-traditional workflow, or will it likely challenge anything you do?

886. What makes you different or better than others companies selling the same thing?

887. What is the average size of your matters in an applicable measurement?

888. Who will be given a copy of this document and where will it be kept?

889. What are the cost implications?

890. What was the rationale for the decision?

891. Do strategies and tactics aimed at less than full control reduce the costs of management or simply shift the cost burden?

892. What is the line where eDiscovery ends and document review begins?

3.5 Quality Audit: Video Communication

893. How does the organization know that its industry and community engagement planning and management systems are appropriately effective and constructive in enabling relationships with key stakeholder groups?

894. Are training programs documented?

895. How does your organization know that its staff are presenting original work, and properly acknowledging the work of others?

896. Are measuring and test equipment that have been placed out of service suitably identified and excluded from use in any device reconditioning operation?

897. Is there a written procedure for receiving materials?

898. It is inappropriate to seek information about the Audit Panels preliminary views including questions like why do you ask that?

899. How does your organization know that the review processes are effective?

900. How does your organization know that its relationships with relevant professional bodies are appropriately effective and constructive?

901. How does your organization know that its system for managing intellectual property issues is appropriately effective, constructive and fair?

902. Is there any content that may be legally actionable?

903. How does your organization know that its relationships with industry and employers are appropriately effective and constructive?

904. How does your organization know that its relationships with the community at large are appropriately effective and constructive?

905. How does your organization know that its system for recruiting the best staff possible are appropriately effective and constructive?

906. How does your organization know that its staff have appropriate access to a fair and effective grievance process?

907. How does your organization know that its staff support services planning and management systems are appropriately effective and constructive?

908. Have the risks associated with the intentions been identified, analyzed and appropriate responses developed?

909. Has a written procedure been established to identify devices during all stages of receipt, reconditioning, distribution and installation so that mix-ups are prevented?

910. What are the main things that hinder your ability to do a good job?

911. Is refuse and garbage adequately stored and disposed of with sufficient frequency to prevent contamination?

912. How does your organization know that its Governance system is appropriately effective and constructive?

3.6 Team Directory: Video Communication

913. Where should the information be distributed?

914. Is construction on schedule?

915. What are you going to deliver or accomplish?

916. When does information need to be distributed?

917. How does the team resolve conflicts and ensure tasks are completed?

918. Who will write the meeting minutes and distribute?

919. How do unidentified risks impact the outcome of the Video Communication project?

920. How will you accomplish and manage the objectives?

921. Where will the product be used and/or delivered or built when appropriate?

922. Process decisions: how well was task order work performed?

923. Days from the time the issue is identified?

924. Process decisions: are all start-up, turn over and close out requirements of the contract satisfied?

925. Who are your stakeholders (customers, sponsors, end users, team members)?

926. How and in what format should information be presented?

927. Contract requirements complied with?

928. Process decisions: do job conditions warrant additional actions to collect job information and document on-site activity?

929. Does a Video Communication project team directory list all resources assigned to the Video Communication project?

930. Decisions: is the most suitable form of contract being used?

3.7 Team Operating Agreement: Video Communication

931. Do you send out the agenda and meeting materials in advance?

932. Conflict resolution: how will disputes and other conflicts be mediated or resolved?

933. Confidentiality: how will confidential information be handled?

934. How will your group handle planned absences?

935. How do you want to be thought of and known within your organization?

936. What is the anticipated procedure (recruitment, solicitation of volunteers, or assignment) for selecting team members?

937. How will you divide work equitably?

938. Do you record meetings for the already stated unable to attend?

939. What are some potential sources of conflict among team members?

940. Are leadership responsibilities shared among team members (versus a single leader)?

941. Are there more than two national cultures

represented by your team?

942. Do you solicit member feedback about meetings and what would make them better?

943. Must your members collaborate successfully to complete Video Communication projects?

944. What is culture?

945. What are the boundaries (organizational or geographic) within which you operate?

946. How will group handle unplanned absences?

947. Are there more than two functional areas represented by your team?

948. Do you ask participants to close laptops and place mobile devices on silent on the table while the meeting is in progress?

949. What is a Virtual Team?

950. Do team members need to frequently communicate as a full group to make timely decisions?

3.8 Team Performance Assessment: Video Communication

951. To what degree do team members articulate the teams work approach?

952. To what degree do members articulate the goals beyond the team membership?

953. How do you encourage members to learn from each other?

954. To what degree are the members clear on what they are individually responsible for and what they are jointly responsible for?

955. To what degree are the teams goals and objectives clear, simple, and measurable?

956. How do you keep key people outside the group informed about its accomplishments?

957. To what degree does the teams work approach provide opportunity for members to engage in fact-based problem solving?

958. Does more radicalness mean more perceived benefits?

959. What are you doing specifically to develop the leaders around you?

960. To what degree does the teams work approach

provide opportunity for members to engage in results-based evaluation?

961. To what degree do all members feel responsible for all agreed-upon measures?

962. To what degree will the team ensure that all members equitably share the work essential to the success of the team?

963. Social categorization and intergroup behaviour: Does minimal intergroup discrimination make social identity more positive?

964. To what degree can team members vigorously define the teams purpose in considerations with others who are not part of the functioning team?

965. When does the medium matter?

966. If you have criticized someones work for method variance in your role as reviewer, what was the circumstance?

967. To what degree are the goals realistic?

968. How hard do you try to make a good selection?

969. Do you give group members authority to make at least some important decisions?

970. Do friends perform better than acquaintances?

3.9 Team Member Performance Assessment: Video Communication

971. What evaluation results do you have?

972. For what period of time is a member rated?

973. What entity leads the process, selects a potential restructuring option and develops the plan?

974. How was the determination made for which training platforms would be used (i.e., media selection)?

975. What innovations (if any) are developed to realize goals?

976. How is the timing of assessments organized (e.g., pre/post-test, single point during training, multiple reassessment during training)?

977. To what degree does the teams purpose contain themes that are particularly meaningful and memorable?

978. Who they are?

979. Who should attend?

980. What tools are available to determine whether all contract functional and compliance areas of performance objectives, measures, and incentives have been met?

981. What are top priorities?

982. Where can team members go for more detailed information on performance measurement and assessment?

983. What does collaboration look like?

984. What is the role of the Reviewer?

985. What steps have you taken to improve performance?

986. What changes do you need to make to align practices with beliefs?

987. To what degree do the goals specify concrete team work products?

988. What is collaboration?

989. What are the basic principles and objectives of performance measurement and assessment?

3.10 Issue Log: Video Communication

990. Is it a change in scope?

991. What is the status of the issue?

992. What approaches to you feel are the best ones to use?

993. How do you manage human resources?

994. Do you often overlook a key stakeholder or stakeholder group?

995. What is a change?

996. Are the Video Communication project issues uniquely identified, including to which product they refer?

997. Is access to the Issue Log controlled?

998. Who is the issue assigned to?

999. Who reported the issue?

1000. How is this initiative related to other portfolios, programs, or Video Communication projects?

1001. How much time does it take to do it?

1002. Why do you manage human resources?

1003. Do you feel a register helps?

1004. Are the stakeholders getting the information they need, are they consulted, are concerns addressed?

1005. Is the issue log kept in a safe place?

1006. Who is involved as you identify stakeholders?

4.0 Monitoring and Controlling Process Group: Video Communication

1007. What factors are contributing to progress or delay in the achievement of products and results?

1008. Is the program making progress in helping to achieve the set results?

1009. Purpose: toward what end is the evaluation being conducted?

1010. Is there sufficient time allotted between the general system design and the detailed system design phases?

1011. Is the verbiage used appropriate and understandable?

1012. Key stakeholders to work with. How many potential communications channels exist on the Video Communication project?

1013. How many potential communications channels exist on the Video Communication project?

1014. Is there sufficient funding available for this?

1015. Is the program in place as intended?

1016. Is there undesirable impact on staff or resources?

1017. How do you monitor progress?

1018. Use: how will they use the information?

1019. How to ensure validity, quality and consistency?

1020. Did the Video Communication project team have enough people to execute the Video Communication project plan?

1021. When will the Video Communication project be done?

4.1 Project Performance Report: Video Communication

1022. To what degree do team members understand one anothers roles and skills?

1023. To what degree are sub-teams possible or necessary?

1024. To what degree do team members agree with the goals, relative importance, and the ways in which achievement will be measured?

1025. To what degree do individual skills and abilities match task demands?

1026. To what degree do team members frequently explore the teams purpose and its implications?

1027. What is the degree to which rules govern information exchange between groups?

1028. To what degree can the cognitive capacity of individuals accommodate the flow of information?

1029. To what degree is the information network consistent with the structure of the formal organization?

1030. To what degree are the skill areas critical to team performance present?

1031. To what degree are the tasks requirements

reflected in the flow and storage of information?

1032. How can Video Communication project sustainability be maintained?

1033. To what degree does the teams purpose constitute a broader, deeper aspiration than just accomplishing short-term goals?

1034. To what degree is there a sense that only the team can succeed?

1035. To what degree does the formal organization make use of individual resources and meet individual needs?

4.2 Variance Analysis: Video Communication

1036. Is work properly classified as measured effort, LOE, or apportioned effort and appropriately separated?

1037. Other relevant issues of Variance Analysis -selling price or gross margin?

1038. Are material costs reported within the same period as that in which BCWP is earned for that material?

1039. Are work packages assigned to performing organizations?

1040. Budgeted cost for work performed?

1041. Is all contract work included in the CWBS?

1042. How does your organization measure performance?

1043. Who is generally responsible for monitoring and taking action on variances?

1044. Are control accounts opened and closed based on the start and completion of work contained therein?

1045. How are variances affected by multiple material and labor categories?

1046. Are there changes in the overhead pool and/or organization structures?

1047. Are authorized changes being incorporated in a timely manner?

1048. Is work progressively subdivided into detailed work packages as requirements are defined?

1049. Budget versus actual. how does the monthly budget compare to actual experience?

1050. Is data disseminated to the contractors management timely, accurate, and usable?

1051. What can be the cause of an increase in costs?

1052. Is there a logical explanation for any variance?

4.3 Earned Value Status: Video Communication

1053. Are you hitting your Video Communication projects targets?

1054. If earned value management (EVM) is so good in determining the true status of a Video Communication project and Video Communication project its completion, why is it that hardly any one uses it in information systems related Video Communication projects?

1055. When is it going to finish?

1056. Validation is a process of ensuring that the developed system will actually achieve the stakeholders desired outcomes; Are you building the right product? What do you validate?

1057. How does this compare with other Video Communication projects?

1058. What is the unit of forecast value?

1059. Verification is a process of ensuring that the developed system satisfies the stakeholders agreements and specifications; Are you building the product right? What do you verify?

1060. How much is it going to cost by the finish?

1061. Earned value can be used in almost any Video

Communication project situation and in almost any Video Communication project environment. it may be used on large Video Communication projects, medium sized Video Communication projects, tiny Video Communication projects (in cut-down form), complex and simple Video Communication projects and in any market sector. some people, of course, know all about earned value, they have used it for years - but perhaps not as effectively as they could have?

1062. Where are your problem areas?

1063. Where is evidence-based earned value in your organization reported?

4.4 Risk Audit: Video Communication

1064. Has an event time line been developed?

1065. If applicable; does the software interface with new or unproven hardware or unproven vendor products?

1066. What can you do to manage outcomes?

1067. Are team members trained in the use of the tools?

1068. Do you promote education and training opportunities?

1069. What compliance systems do you have in place to address quality, errors, and outcomes?

1070. Do you have a mechanism for managing change?

1071. Are you meeting your legal, regulatory and compliance requirements - if not, why not?

1072. Do you have written and signed agreements/contracts in place for each paid staff member?

1073. Are audit program plans risk-adjusted?

1074. Does your auditor understand your business?

1075. Have customers been involved fully in the definition of requirements?

1076. Is the customer willing to participate in reviews?

1077. What are the boundaries of the auditors responsibility for policing management fidelity?

1078. Are procedures in place to ensure the security of staff and information and compliance with privacy legislation if applicable?

1079. Is all expenditure authorised through an identified process?

1080. Do requirements put excessive performance constraints on the product?

1081. Is there (or should there be) some impact on the process of setting materiality when the auditor more effectively identifies higher risk areas of the financial statements?

1082. Is safety information provided to all involved?

4.5 Contractor Status Report: Video Communication

1083. How is risk transferred?

1084. Are there contractual transfer concerns?

1085. If applicable; describe your standard schedule for new software version releases. Are new software version releases included in the standard maintenance plan?

1086. How does the proposed individual meet each requirement?

1087. What are the minimum and optimal bandwidth requirements for the proposed solution?

1088. What was the budget or estimated cost for your organizations services?

1089. Describe how often regular updates are made to the proposed solution. Are corresponding regular updates included in the standard maintenance plan?

1090. Who can list a Video Communication project as organization experience, your organization or a previous employee of your organization?

1091. What process manages the contracts?

1092. What was the actual budget or estimated cost for your organizations services?

1093. What was the overall budget or estimated cost?

1094. How long have you been using the services?

1095. What is the average response time for answering a support call?

1096. What was the final actual cost?

4.6 Formal Acceptance: Video Communication

1097. Was the Video Communication project goal achieved?

1098. What is the Acceptance Management Process?

1099. Who would use it?

1100. Was the Video Communication project managed well?

1101. Do you perform formal acceptance or burn-in tests?

1102. Do you buy pre-configured systems or build your own configuration?

1103. Do you buy-in installation services?

1104. Have all comments been addressed?

1105. What can you do better next time?

1106. Was the client satisfied with the Video Communication project results?

1107. General estimate of the costs and times to complete the Video Communication project?

1108. What are the requirements against which to test, Who will execute?

1109. Did the Video Communication project achieve its MOV?

1110. Did the Video Communication project manager and team act in a professional and ethical manner?

1111. Is formal acceptance of the Video Communication project product documented and distributed?

1112. What was done right?

1113. What function(s) does it fill or meet?

1114. Was the sponsor/customer satisfied?

1115. How well did the team follow the methodology?

1116. Does it do what client said it would?

5.0 Closing Process Group: Video Communication

1117. Is this an updated Video Communication project Proposal Document?

1118. Did the Video Communication project management methodology work?

1119. Did you do what you said you were going to do?

1120. Can the lesson learned be replicated?

1121. How critical is the Video Communication project success to the success of your organization?

1122. Were the outcomes different from the already stated planned?

1123. When will the Video Communication project be done?

1124. Did you do things well?

1125. Will the Video Communication project deliverable(s) replace a current asset or group of assets?

1126. Mitigate. what will you do to minimize the impact should a risk event occur?

1127. How well did the team follow the chosen processes?

1128. What is the amount of funding and what Video Communication project phases are funded?

1129. What areas does the group agree are the biggest success on the Video Communication project?

1130. What is the Video Communication project name and date of completion?

1131. How well did the chosen processes produce the expected results?

1132. Were cost budgets met?

5.1 Procurement Audit: Video Communication

1133. Has guidelines been set up for how the procurement function/unit should carry out its procurements?

1134. Are there procedures for trade-in arrangements?

1135. Does your organization have an overall procurement strategy and/or policy?

1136. Does the strategy discus the best manner of purchase, considering the types of goods and services needed?

1137. Does procurement staff have skills to procure complex or special items (i.e. IT)?

1138. Are the official minutes written in a clear and concise manner?

1139. Does an appropriately qualified official check the quality of performance against the contract terms?

1140. Was timely and equal access to contract documents and information provided to all candidates?

1141. Are behaviour modification applied to change procurement of goods and services if procurement is not functioning properly?

1142. Is there no evidence that the expert has influenced the decisions taken by the public authority in his/her interest or in the interest of a specific contractor?

1143. Are all checks stored in a secure area?

1144. Are reports based on sound data available to the already stated responsible for monitoring the performance of contracts?

1145. Was confidentiality ensured when necessary?

1146. If the expert was allowed to submit a tender, was all the relevant information the expert had gained from his earlier involvement made available to the other bidders?

1147. Were results of the award procedures published?

1148. Are checks safeguarded against theft, loss, or misuse?

1149. Did the chosen procedure ensure competition and transparency?

1150. Is trend analysis performed on expenditures made by key employees and by vendor?

1151. Could bidders learn all relevant information straight from the tender documents?

5.2 Contract Close-Out: Video Communication

1152. Have all acceptance criteria been met prior to final payment to contractors?

1153. What is capture management?

1154. Parties: who is involved?

1155. Change in attitude or behavior?

1156. Has each contract been audited to verify acceptance and delivery?

1157. Have all contracts been closed?

1158. Was the contract complete without requiring numerous changes and revisions?

1159. Have all contract records been included in the Video Communication project archives?

1160. How is the contracting office notified of the automatic contract close-out?

1161. What happens to the recipient of services?

1162. Are the signers the authorized officials?

1163. Have all contracts been completed?

1164. Change in circumstances?

1165. Parties: Authorized?

1166. How does it work?

1167. Was the contract sufficiently clear so as not to result in numerous disputes and misunderstandings?

1168. Change in knowledge?

1169. How/when used ?

1170. Was the contract type appropriate?

5.3 Project or Phase Close-Out: Video Communication

1171. Were risks identified and mitigated?

1172. What were the goals and objectives of the communications strategy for the Video Communication project?

1173. Did the Video Communication project management methodology work?

1174. Who controlled the resources for the Video Communication project?

1175. Complete yes or no?

1176. What went well?

1177. Who is responsible for award close-out?

1178. What process was planned for managing issues/ risks?

1179. Does the lesson describe a function that would be done differently the next time?

1180. What is the information level of detail required for each stakeholder?

1181. What were the actual outcomes?

1182. What advantages do the an individual interview

have over a group meeting, and vice-versa?

1183. What security considerations needed to be addressed during the procurement life cycle?

1184. What benefits or impacts does the stakeholder group expect to obtain as a result of the Video Communication project?

1185. Is the lesson significant, valid, and applicable?

1186. Was the user/client satisfied with the end product?

1187. What stakeholder group needs, expectations, and interests are being met by the Video Communication project?

1188. What was learned?

1189. Were messages directly related to the release strategy or phases of the Video Communication project?

5.4 Lessons Learned: Video Communication

1190. What data are likely to be missing?

1191. Was any formal risk assessment carried out at the start of the Video Communication project, and was this followed up during the Video Communication project?

1192. What is (are) the indicator(s) of success?

1193. Who has execution authority?

1194. Whom to share Lessons Learned Information with?

1195. How much communication is task-related?

1196. Were the right people available when required?

1197. What is the frequency of communication?

1198. Are there any data that you have overlooked in identifying lessons?

1199. What would you approach differently next time?

1200. What skills did you need that were missing on this Video Communication project?

1201. What is the impact of tax policy on the case?

1202. How effective were Video Communication project audits?

1203. How complete and timely were the materials you were provided to decide whether to proceed from one Video Communication project lifecycle phase to the next?

1204. How well do you feel the executives supported this Video Communication project?

1205. What rewards do the individuals seek?

1206. What is your strategy for data collection?

1207. Where do you go from here?

1208. What worked well/did not work well?

1209. How spontaneous are the communications?

Index

motivation   25, 101
motive 188
movement   170
moving   112
multiple   141, 202, 234, 242
mutual 134
narrow 61
national   132, 230
nature 54
nearest   11
nearly 109
necessary   64-65, 71, 90, 118, 124, 134-135, 180, 183, 198,
213, 222, 240, 255
needed   17-18, 20-23, 25-26, 41, 64-65, 93, 102-103, 139,
177, 179, 187, 190, 194, 196, 207-208, 210, 213-214, 254, 259
negotiated   116, 214
neither 1
nervous   140
network   3, 163, 240
Neutral 10, 15, 27, 44, 59, 75, 92, 104
normal 92, 170
Notice 1
notified   198, 256
number   26, 42, 58, 74, 91, 103, 125, 167, 169, 262
numbers   114
numerous   256-257
objection   16, 21
objective   7, 53, 130, 198, 207
objectives   20, 25, 27, 34, 65, 70, 94, 97, 105, 116, 128, 174,
182, 194-195, 206-207, 217, 228, 232, 234-235, 258
observe   192
observed   89
observing   211
obsolete   113
obstacles   18, 171, 179
obtain 207, 259
obtained   28, 183
obtaining   49
obviously   10
occurrence   198
occurring   88
occurs 16, 52, 102, 134, 186
offerings   62, 88

CPSIA information can be obtained
at www.ICGtesting.com
Printed in the USA
BVHW041011200819
556236BV00011B/738/P